BEYOND
THE SUN

COART RAMEY

Bob Jones University Press, Greenville, South Carolina 29614

This textbook was written by members of the faculty and staff of Bob Jones University. Standing for the "old-time-religion" and the absolute authority of the Bible since 1927, Bob Jones University is the world's leading Fundamentalist Christian university. The staff of the University is devoted to educating Christian men and women to be servants of Jesus Christ in all walks of life.

Providing unparalleled academic excellence, Bob Jones University prepares its students through its offering of over one hundred majors, while its fervent spiritual emphasis prepares their minds and hearts for service and devotion to the Lord Jesus Christ.

If you would like more information about the spiritual and academic opportunities available at Bob Jones University, please call *1-800-BJ-AND-ME* (1-800-252-6363). www.bju.edu

NOTE:

The fact that materials produced by other publishers may be referred to in this volume does not constitute an endorsement by Bob Jones University Press of the content or theological position of materials produced by such publishers. The position of Bob Jones University Press, and the University itself, is well known. Any references and ancillary materials are listed as an aid to the student or the teacher and in an attempt to maintain the accepted academic standards of the publishing industry.

Beyond the Sun

Coart Ramey, M.A.

Editor: Thomas Parr
Designer: Noelle Snyder
Cover designers: John Bjerk and Elly Kalagayan
Composition: Carol Larson

© 2001 Bob Jones University Press
Greenville, South Carolina 29614

Printed in the United States of America
All rights reserved

ISBN 1-57924-616-8

15 14 13 12 11 10 9 8 7 6 5 4 3 2 1

CONTENTS

*I*ntroduction v

*B*lack Sheep Book? 1

*I*nfinite Desire, Infinite Provision . . . 17

A Heart for Eternity 37

*O*aths and Tragedies. 51

*L*ife from the Long View 65

*T*his Slippery, Tricky Life We Live. . . 81

*R*ejoice and Remember. 93

Wisdom's Delight

Jerusalem, about 940 B.C.

Pillars of stone, pillars of cedar, and pillars of bronze succeeded each other from the massive gateway across the mosaic courtyard to the Royal Porch. Seven ornate bronze columns towered over the guards, who saluted in recognition. Up the eight steps and into the cool shade I went and nodded at Kadir, who vanished into the darkened interior. I remember some slight qualm as he announced my name, though I had no way of knowing what would be special about this occasion.

I walked inside and along the partition wall. Two steps past its end, I kept my eyes straight ahead before turning smartly to my left. There was the familiar grandeur of the throne, like a giant golden peacock backed against the far wall. Windows and skylights cast daylight upon the assembled courtiers. Even as the king bade me approach, I scanned for some irregularity in their faces. The shallower, sillier fellows looked bored or distracted, but my friends were all grave, some downcast.

Most somber of all was the king. "Hokmah," said he, "you must grant me what no one can!" Surprised he had spoken first, I quickly responded with a request to know his will, bowing nearly to the paving stones. "These greatest of advisors, at whose disposal I have placed all the learning of the world, have failed me!" His voice cracked, and he was silent for a moment.

"Hokmah, I have looked everywhere under the sun. I explored the depths of everything man can do, and often you have helped me. You have shown me how to reach higher, farther, and deeper than any other king ever has. You have helped me see the pattern of the stars and the perfection of the lily flower. You have filled my soul again and again. But *that is the curse!*"

You will understand, I hope, some of the swirl of fear, pity, sadness, sympathy, and confusion I felt at these words. Or perhaps you will not, for I perceive that not all peoples in all times know what it is to have a king as we do. I was the servant to this good king, a gift given to him by God, and it was my duty to find ways to accomplish his every wish. I had always done this, but still he found cause for discontent.

"Make known to me your heart, king and friend, and as ever I will offer the way of God," I requested. He actually rose from the throne, with a look of grief on him.

"All I seek is to be full. I know how to enjoy food and drink, and love and music. I know more of the ways of this world than any other man. I have built more and of greater beauty than any before me. But still I am not satisfied!" He turned his eyes fully on me, and his voice almost pleaded. "What desire must I quench to make me full? Is this all that life is, a quest that I cannot complete, though I journey on with every year I live? It is you, Hokmah, who have taken me so high, only to leave me longing to go higher still. It is you who have taught me goodness, but given me no power to cleanse the evil from men. It is you who have opened to me a world, only to leave me wondering if there are not more worlds to know and perhaps to build myself. But life will fail me first!"

The king strode heavily down the steps to his throne, coming directly before me. I bowed low to the ground as he spoke again. "Lady Hokmah, are you in truth a blessing, or a curse?"

"O great king," I began softly, "forgive me for taking joy in what is to you sorrow. But if you will hear me, you will know the reason.

"Know, my king, that your present grief is in the purpose of God, and its accomplishment my charge from God. Yet it is not an end," I quickly added, "but only the gateway into a holy palace. I have guided you in meeting your every desire, but now, my king, it is granted you to see the greatest truth. Only by your disappointment could you win the treasure God sought to give you. Only despair could prepare you for the completion of my service to you. And now all men forever may learn of me from you." The king turned soberly and remounted the steps to his throne. Looking profoundly tired, he motioned me to continue.

● ● ●

Hokmah is the Hebrew word for wisdom. What Hokmah taught King Solomon after his great frustration he recorded for us in the Bible. We have a book about life from a king who had a unique ability to explore life and to view it with God's wisdom.

Do you ever get tired of trying to learn all there is to learn? It seems like school always has another subject to discuss, another level to that subject, and a mass of details to memorize. Outside of school are the thousands of things you have to learn to be a successful adult: personal finance, dealing with coworkers, making a good marriage, raising children, choosing and mastering a life's calling, and finding the right church to join and grow in.

Life itself can be intimidating. Problems and hardships fill the lives of most adults, even Christian adults. In the world at large, everyone seems to be striving for something no one ever finds. Many invest their lives to make money. Wealthy people are rarely  happy, though; they are as much or more likely than others to have miserable personal lives. The wealth they work for can be snatched away by unforeseen circumstances, and eventually death snatches them away from their wealth.

The Bible deals with all of these problems, but one book in particular wrestles with a godly philosophy of life. Your philosophy, the mix of background knowledge and ethical standards you use to make decisions, determines the course of your life. You have a philosophy of life whether or not you ever planned one. It is the map by which you will steer your life for years ahead.

God wants us to have a certain philosophy of life that pleases and glorifies Him. More than the sum of His individual commandments, it is the set of principles that you and I have to apply to our own unique situations in order to make the right choices. Often, it has surprising components; for example, God's philosophy of life for us touches on money, recreation, adventure, labor, love, government, suffering, and a host of other things.

The book that explains the God-pleasing philosophy of life is Ecclesiastes. Solomon, son of David, king of God's chosen nation Israel, and by God's gift the wisest mere man who ever lived, wrote Ecclesiastes. He addressed the book to all people in all time, not just Israelites and not just godly people. But he meant the book especially for young people. Young people have one major power: their whole lives lie ahead of them to shape as they choose. More than older people, who have already spent a significant part of their lives, young people need the godly philosophy of life so that they can direct their *entire* lives to go God's way.

Young people in Solomon's day faced the same problems and temptations you do. Under the inspiration of the Holy Spirit, the king sought to impart divine wisdom, ripened over a lifetime, in such a way as to tell them why life is like it is and what they should do in response. If, like most young people, you have always wanted someone to tell you how to have a happy and fulfilling life, you will enjoy a study of Ecclesiastes. The answers you want are in God's Word because the Lord God will never let you down.

CHAPTER ONE

Black Sheep Book?

1

Memory Verses: Ecclesiastes 12:13-14

Ecclesiastes may be the most misunderstood and maligned book of the Bible. One reason for the misunderstanding is the difficulty of bringing certain terms accurately into English. Another reason is the inherent difficulty of the book, even when it is perfectly translated. We want to look first at a number of terms that have to be correctly understood before the message of the book will be clear, and then we want to look at the broader misinterpretations of the philosophy of Ecclesiastes.

Connotations

Ecclesiastes was written in ancient Hebrew a thousand years before the birth of Christ (three thousand years ago) in a foreign country in a very different culture. If you have ever learned a modern foreign language, such as Spanish or German, you know that it is impossible to translate *exactly* from one language to another. Grammar differs, idioms and figures of speech do not cross over, and the connotations of words and phrases cannot be included in simple translation.

Connotations are the thoughts and emotions a word conjures up in your mind even though they are not really part of that word's meaning. For example, *spider* means an arachnid with an unsegmented body and spinnerets for making web. It does not mean scary, or creepy, or interesting, or fun, though different people may think any of those things when they hear "spider." These are the *connotations* of the word, in contrast to its definition, or *denotation*.

A spider also serves to illustrate the kind of connotations we are most concerned about. There are various kinds of connotations, but to study Ecclesiastes we need to be aware of **emotive connotations**, or the emotions that something arouses in you. It is important to notice the difference between **positive, negative,** and **neutral emotive connotations.**

When you have a happy or pleasing thought in response to "spider," you attach a positive emotive connotation to the idea of a spider (even though you may be a bit weird in some people's opinion). Then again, if you feel repulsed or even scared when you hear "spider," you attach a negative emotive connotation to the crea-

ture (and are wimpy in the eyes of the first group). Lastly, if you have no emotional response to the idea of a spider—you couldn't care less if there was a spider anywhere nearby—then you attach a neutral emotive connotation to spiders.

In translating between two languages, connotations cause problems when the word chosen to translate a word in the original language produces the wrong feelings in the readers of the receiver language. Vocabulary very rarely matches perfectly between two languages, so a translator has to make decisions about the appropriate word based on the context of that word in its original language. A wrong choice can cause misunderstanding.

One notable example is the pair of words that can mean either "spirit," "wind," or "breath." In Ecclesiastes and throughout the Old Testament, the word *ruach* is used to mean ordinary wind, breath, the spirit of a man, and the Holy Spirit of God. (To pronounce *ruach,* say "roo" as in a kangaroo and then "akh," making the last sound high in your throat like a hiss, or what you do when gargling mouthwash.) While you can sense that the relationship between wind and spirit is that both mean something like "unseen force," they are definitely different in the real world. It is usually obvious from context which one is involved, because they are so different they would rarely be interchangeable. One does not expect the Holy Spirit to blow in from the south or the wind of God to enter into a man. The same situation appears in the New Testament, in which the Greek word *pneuma* (the root word for *pneumonia*) can mean either "wind" or "spirit."

However, if an instance occurred in which either meaning could fit the context, a wrong choice on the part of the translator would obscure the intended meaning. Such instances occur in Ecclesiastes. The most important involves a word similar to *ruach,* and another involves a phrase containing *ruach.* The resultant misunderstandings are not really mistakes on the part of translators. The misunderstandings are due mainly to the difficulties with the book as a whole. The translators thought they were choosing terms that fit the overall tone of Ecclesiastes, when a literal translation would have better served the meaning.

Key Terms in Ecclesiastes

Most important term: *Vapor*

Most important of all the difficult terms in Ecclesiastes is the one translated "vanity" or "meaninglessness." Both of these English words have negative emotive connotations. When you hear "vanity," you think either of someone who is arrogantly proud of his own good looks or of some great effort that fails to accomplish its goal. But the underlying word literally means "vapor," as in steam or mist. It is often used as a picture of things that are empty or worthless; for example, idols are often called "vapor" because there is nothing really to them.

When you read in Ecclesiastes, "Life is vanity," it sounds very negative, even depressing. But if you read it, "Life is vapor," what emotion do you feel? What message do you get? To call life (or anything else) *vapor* is to make a **metaphor,** a figure of speech in which a writer states that one thing *is* another, not because it is literally true, but because there is some point of similarity between the two things. For instance, if I were to say, "My wife is a jewel," I am making a metaphor. I do not intend to communicate that everything true of a jewel is true of my wife. I do not mean to say that she is hard, cutting, and expensive. I mean that she is very rare and precious and a prized possession to me. If you overheard me in a conversation praising my wife and heard me insert this metaphor, you would know by context what point of similarity between my wife and a jewel I had in mind.

Every time you read that something is vapor, think about the point of similarity that the author has in mind. Do not try to make everything about vapor true of the thing called vapor. For example, "life is vapor" does not mean that life is always getting higher and thinner (whatever that would mean). Most of the time the idea is transience. Transient things are temporary, passing, and impermanent. Be careful not to imagine negative connotations when the author did not intend any.

Other key terms

Vexation of spirit translates a Hebrew phrase that is literally "chasing wind." As mentioned above, the same Hebrew word is used for both "wind" and "spirit." As with vapor, the phrase deals with pursuing things that are transitory and impermanent. The wind is certainly real, and you can chase it if you want to, but no one can catch and keep the wind. Chasing wind is bound to be a fruitless and frustrating endeavor.

Under the sun shows us that the book speaks in the realm of earthly life, not the life to come. It does not deny eternal life any more than do the Ten Commandments; in fact, ancient Near Eastern peoples universally assumed the afterlife. We can see the underlying assumption of eternal life with God showing through in several places in Ecclesiastes. But the author's quest, counsel, and resolution are all located in this present earthly life.

Hate is not an emotional reaction but an act of the will, a choice. Hate means to reject. It is the opposite of *love*, which means to choose or accept. When the Preacher finds life unable to provide permanent, satisfying good, he "hates" it, or rejects it as the solution to his search. Emotion may be involved, but the Hebrew words do not have the pure emotive connotations of their modern English equivalents.

Profit is the remainder or leftover from earthly life. It is not a term for heavenly reward, but a reference to the impermanence of all material things. No "profit" under the sun means that nothing material in this life carries over into the next (see 5:15-16). In English, *profit* nearly always has a positive emotive connotation (we all love to make a profit in business). *Remainder,* which is basically neutral, is a more accurate word.

Portion refers to the measure of rightful wealth or happiness that God gives to a man during his earthly life. A man's portion provides routine satisfaction to make life enjoyable. God gives a portion to saved and unsaved people alike as a sign of his goodness. The portion is part of the vapor of life, but it is good, not evil.

Fool is the term for someone who is willfully ignorant of the right way and rebellious against God. We think of the English term applying to someone who is mentally deficient, but the biblical fool may be educated and highly intelligent. In contrast is the *wise one,* a person who submits to God's will and does what is right.

Author of Ecclesiastes

In this book, the author of Ecclesiastes will often be referred to as "The Preacher," a good translation of the title *(qoheleth)* he takes for himself. Though Chapter 2 will explain more fully why the author of Ecclesiastes was almost certainly King Solomon, it will suffice for now to observe that the author claims an identity that could only apply to Solomon (1:12) and that the circumstantial evidence fits Solomon far better than anyone else. Solomon was the wisest of men, he wrote other biblical wisdom literature that resembles Ecclesiastes, and he more than any other had the capacity to do the things the Preacher claimed to do.

Universal Appeal of Ecclesiastes

King Solomon wrote Ecclesiastes in a style that was familiar in the ancient Near East. Solomon lived about a thousand years before Christ, a time when civilization in the Near East (what we now call the Middle East, the land spanning Egypt, Israel, Jordan, Syria, Lebanon, Turkey, and Iraq) was at a high point. Society was very stratified, meaning that there were definite social classes into which people fell. Generally speaking, you were born into a class and stayed in it for life.

The highest class was a group of educated leaders, mostly men, who were the governors, generals, priests, and other top officials.

Think About It!

A Sample of Egyptian Wisdom Literature

Guard thyself against robbing the oppressed
And against overbearing the disabled.
Stretch not forth thy hand against the approach of an old man,
Nor *steal away* the speech of the *aged*.

Let not thyself be sent on a dangerous errand,
Nor love him who carries it out.
Do not cry out against him whom thou hast attacked,
Nor return him answer on thy own behalf.

He who does evil, the (very) river-band abandons him,
And his *floodwaters* carry him off.
The north wind comes down that it may end his hour;
It is joined to the tempest;
The thunder is loud, and the crocodiles are wicked.

"The Instruction of Amen-em-opet," trans. John A. Wilson. *Ancient Near Eastern Texts Relating to the Old Testament*, ed. James B. Pritchard (Princeton, NJ: Princeton Univ. Press, 1950.)

These men had to be carefully trained in the ways of life if they were to contribute successfully to the operation of the nation. To aid their training, older leaders wrote wisdom literature. Wisdom literature was instruction in right living and wise behavior. We have sample wisdom literature from other nations at the time, such as Egypt.

Wisdom literature came in two types: didactic, consisting of strings of wise sayings and admonitions, and reflective, essays by wise men giving advice to the young based on their own life experiences. The Bible contains samples of both types. Most of Proverbs is didactic wisdom literature, while Job and Ecclesiastes are reflective wisdom literature.

Bible wisdom literature followed the same style as contemporary wisdom literature, but it was quite different in substance. People in other countries would have recognized Ecclesiastes as a sample of reflective wisdom literature and read it to find out King Solomon's advice about life. Solomon was a spectacularly famous king by the end of his reign. Scripture tells us that people, even other monarchs, came from all around to seek Solomon's wisdom and see his marvelous accomplishments.

A book authored by the great King Solomon would have commanded international attention. Solomon apparently intended to address both godly and ungodly people with this book. It appears at first to be similar to other wisdom literature—part of the reason it is hard to reconcile with the rest of the Bible. As to its philosophy, wisdom literature tended to be at odds with the one true God. It was often fatalistic and humanistic. However, Solomon's book surprises the reader by subtly but deftly turning his mind away from the world and onto God. At first it seems pessimistic, but in time proves itself entirely optimistic because it focuses on God. Ecclesiastes has to be read and digested, but the nourishment it gives is an exhortation to faith in Almighty God.

Ecclesiastes, therefore, was effectively a tract to the rich and educated. It came in a form of literature they recognized and engaged their minds with its challenging presentation. It spoke to them at their level. Life's pleasures and pursuits took up so much of their time and energy that they could relate to the Preacher and his search for lasting value.

Moreover, it was a tract to the young everywhere. Youth are especially susceptible to falling for the world's empty promises. Solomon teaches them the truth to life and points them toward what they really want, even if they do not know it.

Nevertheless, Ecclesiastes speaks to every individual regardless of age or status. It deals with the stuff of real life. Life's hardships, worries, disappointments, and frustrations are familiar to all people. Solomon offers wisdom that everyone needs. The godly will appreciate far more what God Himself means to them from a study of Ecclesiastes. The ungodly will face a choice either to turn their life to the pursuit of God or to continue living their brief lives for the sake of vapor.

Special Sections

"Epicurean" Refrains

Three times in Ecclesiastes occurs a short passage often called an "Epicurean" refrain (2:24-26; 5:20; 8:15). A refrain is just a line repeated at points throughout a song or poem, as most songs have. But *Epicurean* refers to a philosophy based on the teachings of Epicurus, a Greek philosopher of the third century B.C.

Epicurus taught that pain was equivalent to evil and pleasure was equivalent to good. He rejected the idea that the gods (let alone the true God) were involved in human affairs, and he did not believe in any life after death. Epicurus himself did not advocate a wild abandonment to sensual pleasure but taught moderate enjoyment of good things in a peaceable, friend-filled lifestyle.

If you scan the three passages listed above, you will see why they are called "Epicurean." There is some semblance between Ecclesiastes and Epicurus. However, two major points make it impossible that King Solomon was an Epicurean. First and foremost, Solomon died six hundred years before Epicurus was born. The only way to see Epicurean influence is to deny that Solomon wrote Ecclesiastes despite the strong evidence that he did. Second, the philosophy of Ecclesiastes is not Epicurean, despite the refrains. It assumes eternal life and a living, righteous God who will judge all men for their work in this life.

Solomon was a famous wise man in his day even in the world outside of Israel, thanks to the wisdom God had given him. Epicurus was a learned, cosmopolitan Greek in the time when Jews had been scattered from Canaan across the ancient world. Epicurus may well have come in contact with religious Jews and read some of their Scriptures, including the wisdom literature.

As we will see, even though Ecclesiastes appeals to unsaved people, it is very difficult for an ungodly person to properly understand. Since Epicurus borrowed other parts of his philosophy from predecessors, such as the Greek philosopher Democritus, it is no stretch to suppose he may have developed his philosophy of pleasure from an imperfect understanding (or an incomplete acceptance) of Ecclesiastes.

The so-called Epicurean refrains serve an important function within the Book of Ecclesiastes. They are not pagan in philosophy, but godly and wholesome. But we have to take them in context to understand them.

Wisdom Sections

Throughout Ecclesiastes King Solomon sprinkled wisdom sayings that sound like the Book of Proverbs. These are surprising and sometimes hard to fit into the rest of the book. For now, keep in mind that the wisdom sections teach about how to deal with this life—that is, mortal earthly life in contrast to eternal life with God. Proverbs is the same way, of course, but in Proverbs you have nothing but masses of wisdom sayings without the surrounding context of an essay on life. Ecclesiastes incorporates wisdom sayings into its singular overall message. While any wisdom saying means something by itself, just as in Proverbs, within Ecclesiastes every wisdom saying is amplified by its place in the book as a whole.

Structure of Ecclesiastes

To understand any written composition, it helps to know its structure. Anything worth writing will follow an orderly, logical plan of some kind. This is why magazine articles have section breaks, why books have chapters listed in a table of contents, why both have paragraphs and punctuated sentences, and why even poetry has lines and stanzas. Your brain understands faster what it has help subdividing and organizing.

Cyclical nature of the literature

Solomon did not organize Ecclesiastes in any way that is familiar to us. Stephen Langton, Archbishop of Canterbury, separated the Bible into chapters during the thirteenth century. Please do not think of Solomon as having twelve main points to cover in each of the twelve chapters in Ecclesiastes, or you will get very confused.

In the modern western world we are accustomed to essays progressing sequentially; that is, main ideas come one at a time in a logical order and the subpoints develop within each main idea in a logical order. There is not supposed to be any overlap of ideas unless the author was incompetent. The skill of outlining is necessary, and a good essay is just a filled-in outline.

But ancient literature does not have to conform to our ways of thinking. Oh, they have to be logical and orderly to be valuable, but they do *not* have to progress sequentially. Much ancient literature, including much in our Bible, follows a more artistic plan. A logical outline is in the author's mind, but he writes in cycles, presenting most or all of the main ideas in skeletal form once, then going back through them, again and again, elaborating certain points to strengthen and eventually complete his supporting arguments.

Such an arrangement lends itself well to reading and remembering an essay because it lets the reader see how the main points connect to each other as each one is steadily strengthened. In the sequential system, one main point is exhausted and then abandoned, making it more difficult for the reader to keep in mind how the next main point relates to the first and how both support the theme of the essay. Ecclesiastes follows a cyclical pattern.

Overall Outline

Because of the nature of the literature, Ecclesiastes is notoriously difficult to outline in the conventional sense. Solomon probably could have outlined it well. We can only observe what he wrote and try to describe it with an outline. The only reason we even try is to clarify our own understanding of the book. The best way to master the book is to read it over and over again.

There is no general consensus among scholars as to the right way to outline Ecclesiastes. We will adopt a convenient scheme based on the concept of cyclical literature, the three Epicurean refrains, and the tendency of cyclical literature to have parallel elements before and after the middle of the book.

Notice that the three refrains generally divide the book into three parts. The first refrain *ends* the first section, the second refrain is in the *middle* of the second section, and the third refrain *begins* the third section. Chapters 3 and 7 essentially mirror each other, as do chapters 4 and 6. Chapter 5 is the central chapter. The quest in Chapter 2 is answered by the climax in 11:7–12:12. The introduction and conclusion complement each other effectively.

As we study the book of Ecclesiastes, we will refer to this outline after every chapter in order to keep our bearings. You need to keep the entire book in mind to see how the individual parts contribute to the whole.

Outline of Ecclesiastes   Refrains

Introduction: Theme stated—all is vapor 1:1-3

Illustration: Endless repetition in nature 1:4-11

The Preacher fails in his quest because life is transient, but he realizes God has given this life for temporary enjoyment, not permanent satisfaction. 1:12–2:26   2:24

Times poem: God arranges everything as it should be. Preview of subthemes. 3:1-22

- Wisdom is paramount in spite of human failure. 4:1-16

- Wisdom is paramount, so fear God! 5:1-20   5:20

- Earthly life is transient. 6:1-12

Wisdom poem: Human failure persists despite the superiority of wisdom. 7:1-29

God is the solution to the problem that life is transient. 8:1–9:10   8:15

Wisdom is paramount but inadequate due to sin. 9:11–11:6

Climax: Rejoice and Remember. 11:7–12:1

Old age removes the ability to enjoy life and serve God. 12:2-8

Conclusion: Fear God! 12:9-14

Review and Discussion

1. Imagine you are preparing a translator's handbook. Your task is to be sure that the translator understands the emotion attached to English words so that he can successfully render the following selection into Mandarin Chinese. Identify three words or phrases with emotive connotations that could potentially cause misunderstandings. Write each one in the space provided along with a short explanation of what the author meant and why a non-English speaker might misunderstand.

"Strike Two in Nevada"
by Arno Samuelson

I slid down a rocky embankment under a harsh sky, covering myself in dust. My knees and elbows smarted as I sat up. What had happened this time? Yesterday's mishap on top of Red Bow rock had been bad enough; one more spill like this and I would be heading home. I staggered to my feet and balanced my throbbing watermelon of a head, then walked gingerly back up the bank to see what had become of my bike.

2. In order to see that an English word can have even more meanings than the Hebrew word for "wind," experiment with the range of meanings of the word *run*. What common element can you discern among these four very different uses of *run?* Tell how each use exhibits the common element you see.

"**Run** over to MacroMart and buy us some bread."

"Baltimore puts another **run** on the board!"

"Barbara, you have a terrible **run** in your hose."

"That motor should **run** a lot better now, Mr. Curtis."

3. Imagine you have a friend from India who is learning English. He has written to ask you about five metaphors he came across last week in different things he read. He included his best guess as to the meaning of the metaphor. In the space below, write what you would write to him to explain the *correct* meaning of each metaphor.

"'My love is like a red, red rose.' This means she is thorny and reluctant to grow, yes?"

"'When it came down to it, Corporal Muncy was chicken.' This soldier was fast and worked hard, yes?"

"'All the world's a stage.' This is from when people are thinking the world is flat, yes?"

"'Life was their oyster.' This is to say they are living cold and wet and slimy; they are very unhappy, yes?"

"'To all couch potatoes.' Is this an article to farmers?"

Select the letter of the sentence in which a key term is used *correctly* in each of the following examples.

_____ 4.

    A. Solomon measured his **profit** by his level of annual gold revenue.

    B. To Solomon, a **fool** was someone who knew nothing of the one true God.

    C. Solomon called something **chasing wind** when it was frustratingly fruitless.

_____ 5.

    A. The Preacher says it is wrong to **hate** others.

    B. The Preacher undertakes his quest **under the sun.**

    C. The Preacher considered a man's **portion** to be the burden of suffering for righteousness.

6. Imagine you are Yashir-Qum, a teenage Egyptian nobleman living in 910 B.C. List at least three reasons that you would probably read "The Words of the Preacher" (Ecclesiastes) if it were offered to you.

7. Contrast the strengths of a sequentially ordered essay with those of a cyclically ordered essay.

CHAPTER TWO

Infinite Desire, Infinite Provision

2

Memory Verse: Ecclesiastes 2:26

About the Author

The writer of Ecclesiastes refers to himself as the Preacher or the Speaker, a teacher of wisdom. Often Scripture writers kept themselves completely hidden in the background when their personal identities were irrelevant. The Preacher does not actually give his name. Does he intend that we know who he is, or is he veiling his identity?

In two verses, 1 and 12, he gives information about himself that seems to narrow his identity to only one man. Apparently, the Preacher did expect his readers to know who he was. It would have been impossible for the king of Israel to write anonymously! And only one king of Israel fits the description offered; only Solomon was both son of David and king *over Israel* in Jerusalem. After Solomon's death, the united Israelite kingdom split in two. David's descendants continued to rule Judah from Jerusalem, but Jeroboam's family ruled the northern tribes, which came to be called Israel.

In addition, the book has two strong circumstantial indications that it is Solomon's product. First, only he could justly boast of the extraordinary power to pursue pleasure through any means and still retain great wisdom. No Israelite king ever matched Solomon's wealth or wisdom. Second, the book is wisdom literature, a genre Solomon wrote elsewhere in the Old Testament— certainly parts of the Book of Proverbs and probably the Book of Job and the Song of Solomon.

Altogether, the evidence is solid that King Solomon not only wrote Ecclesiastes but also intended for his readers to know it.

Stating the Theme

A theme is the main idea a writer or speaker has to get across to his audience. Verse 2 expresses the Preacher's theme. The expression "vanity of vanities" means that he is writing about absolute vanity. Think of English phrases like "horror of horrors" and "wonder of wonders" or the Bible's phrase "holy of holies." In none of these is a specific group of horrors or wonders or holies in mind. The thing in question is simply the greatest of its kind, wherever or however many others there may be.

Remembering the real meaning of "vanity," you know that the Preacher wants to tell us about the single greatest "vapor" of all. He wants to teach us this: all is vapor (v. 2). The rhetorical question he raises in verse 3 reinforces the theme: there is NO leftover to any man from all the work he does during his whole life "under the sun." When he departs this life, he takes nothing with him.

We have to get into the Preacher's mind as if this were the first time we had ever read these words. Part of the misunderstanding about his message is due to the fact that his opening is designed to seize the attention of every mortal mind with an assertion everyone instinctively dislikes. We work and sweat every day. We don't *like* to hear that nothing will remain. Consequently, the Preacher gets our attention immediately, even if we are hostile to what he says. I want to hear him prove that all is vapor.

Opening Illustration

Have you ever had a friend try to make you understand something by giving an illustration? Maybe she said something like, "Did you ever watch a puppy see itself in a mirror for the first time? You know how it thinks it sees another dog, so it bristles and

Water Cycle

Verse 7 has sometimes been taken as a description of the hydrologic "water cycle" of precipitation-evaporation-condensation-precipitation, but the Hebrew really just stresses the ceaseless pouring of water into the sea without any rise in sea level. It reads, "To the place the rivers go, there they go again."

growls and barks, just getting madder because the 'other dog' is barking back? Well, that's how I act when I see myself in the mirror each morning, but it's not because I think I'm someone else. It's because I hate how I look!" She could have just said, "I look terrible in the morning" and gone on discussing weightier matters, but she made you really visualize what she meant. The mental image was much more vivid than a simple statement.

The Preacher used the same principle when he opened his discourse on vapor. A natural image is his first attempt to make us comprehend the vapor of vapors. Read his observations in 1:4-7. I can hardly argue with him, of course, but why point out such obvious things? These things have something in common, however; they are all repetitious cycles that, although expending energy unceasingly, never accomplish any permanent change in the world. The cycles are always running but never finishing.

Before you read 8-11, remember that the Preacher is telling us about real life, "under the sun," and is not yet come to a spiritual point. Read these four verses, and think about whether or not you agree with him.

Verse 8 begins the exposition of the Preacher's theme, "all is vapor." He gave an illustration of ceaseless repetition that accomplished nothing permanent. The exposition now states plainly what nature pictures: First, labor is unending and abundant. We all labor and labor daily, but we are never done laboring. We may take breaks and vacations, but the labor always awaits our return. Just like the racing sun and the flowing rivers, labor is a steady cycle of spent energy that doesn't permanently accomplish anything.

Human desire is likewise unceasing, despite continual gratification. The eye sees and ear hears things daily. I get pleasure from seeing beautiful sights and hearing sounds, like music playing or friends talking. Yet never does a day come in which I can say, "That's enough; I need no more. Sights can vanish and sounds can cease. I am satisfied!"

Not only can I not sense anything that finally satisfies me, but neither can I do anything permanently satisfying. This is the meaning of verses 9 and 10, no "new thing" can be done. I can labor and invent and build, but I'll never get enough of it. I always want to do something more. And worse, even though I long to be unique and contribute something special, I find it impossible to do anything that will really last.

I may want to find a cure for cancer, and give all my life's energy to it for years. Maybe I'll even find a cure for some type of cancer and save lives. But, "under the sun," if I live a while, I will see other dread diseases killing people whom I cannot save. New diseases like AIDS arise, some people I save may well turn out to be murderers, and everyone whose life I saved dies anyway sooner or later!

This is the import of the Preacher's observation. It is striking, disturbing, and seems very pessimistic and depressing. But only one question is relevant: Is what he says here the truth?

Solomon's Quest for Fulfillment

Having introduced his theme with an illustration and an exposition, the Preacher drops an autobiographical hint and proceeds to tell the story of this search for satisfaction. Verse 13 records his goal: to search out the meaning of everything in earthly life. I've heard of people doing this before. They set out to determine "the meaning of life." Great philosophers, ancient and recent, have struck the same quest. In a sense, almost every young person searches at some point for meaning in life. The Preacher, King Solomon, even as a boy knew God, and still he was plagued by a desire to understand life. Don't feel guilty if you want to find out what life is all about. It is a natural and worthy question. But there is an answer God Himself has given, and it is here before us in Ecclesiastes to find when we accompany the Preacher on his search.

Solomon's Age

The Bible does not provide any hard data for determining Solomon's age at his succession to the throne. Circumstantial evidence, such as the number of events that took place before and after David's sin with Bathsheba, make it likely that Solomon was born close to the middle of David's forty-year reign. He was therefore probably short of twenty years old when he became king. Solomon also ruled forty years, but would have been no more than sixty when he died—perhaps a victim of the premature aging caused by his excesses.

Solomon was a young man when he assumed the throne of Israel, almost certainly a teenager (see box). We don't know when his search for fulfillment began, but since in verse 16 he refers to his coming to great estate and wisdom, he may well have begun early in his reign. The search he describes would have taken years, even for a great king. Solomon thus records an investigation of the meaning of life that he wants to tell us about. He went where you and I want to go—into the world for adventure and exploration—and now reports his God-directed discoveries.

Having set forth his theme, the Preacher begins to rehearse the search for satisfaction through which he discovered that "all is vapor." This Preacher has told me that everything in earthly life is a mere breath; naturally, I want to know how he came to such a conclusion. He set his heart, or mind, to learn the meaning of everything that happens. This was no small task! He wanted to know the ins and outs of everything in the world, including why people do the things they do, how the natural world works, and how much is possible for a human being to accomplish.

Preliminary Summary

Up front he summarizes his findings: all of it is heavy labor God has given to mankind to occupy them (13). All human works he pronounces vapor and wind-chasing (14). He implies that he really did find out everything done under the sun (though it's hard to believe for the moment) but found it all to be transient, temporary, and passing, just like a puff of air. Working in this world is like chasing the wind—absorbing and aerobic, but hardly able to produce permanent fruit. I immediately wonder, Why has God given us things to do that are ultimately fruitless?

Going on with the preliminary summary of his search, the Preacher declares that every crooked or incomplete thing out there cannot be helped (15). This seems very depressing; I am not sure what he means, so I have to wait for him to cycle back around to it. As you recall from the Introduction, much good literature deals with themes in a cyclic process, bringing up a theme briefly and then going to other themes before returning to elaborate the first one. An author may break up what he has to say on one topic and spread it over three or four (or more) places in his writing. The Psalms and Prophets are especially cyclic, though OT history and even NT books can be cyclic (I John is an example).

This structure is in contrast to a logical outline, in which the author deals with topics one at a time, fully developing each one before going on to the next. Cyclic literature presents different sections of each topic together by showing their relations repeatedly. Imagine an outline that is logically organized this way:

I. Types of ice cream
   A. Hard ice cream
   B. Soft ice cream
II. Flavors of ice cream

　　A. Chocolate
　　B. Vanilla
　III. Ingredients in ice cream
　　A. Milk
　　B. Sugar

presented this way instead:

　IA.　Hard ice cream is the most familiar type.
　IIA.　Chocolate is the most popular flavor.
　IIIA.　Milk is the most needed ingredient.

　IB.　Soft ice cream is also well loved.
　IIB.　Vanilla is admired among purists.
　IIIB.　Sugar is the most important ingredient.

Each main division shows the connections between ideas in its own way. The Preacher uses this cyclical form to explain the different points supporting his theme and message.

Seeking Fulfillment through Learning

In verse 16 King Solomon has a conversation with himself. He says, "Self, you are richer and smarter than anyone has ever been." Now he has to decide what to do with his impressive self. The combination of wisdom, madness, and folly is a poetic device that uses two extremes to represent the entirety of a category. Here, it is another way of saying that he sought out all knowledge, the way of everything [see box on next page]. He devoted all his energy to learning, and declares that it was "chasing wind" (17).

Verse 18 is a great verse to memorize when you are in school. As with everything else the Preacher says, we have to take this statement in context and discern what he really means. Nevertheless, it is true; knowing a lot brings great sorrow! This is not an excuse to stay stupid, but it is a fact of life. (The more you know about the world and the corrupt ways of men, the more reason there is to sorrow.) Even short of that, the labor necessary to amassing knowledge is a great burden. When you sit and sweat over a math test or a history paper, trying to make your brain work, you experience the reality to which our Preacher calls attention.

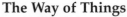

The Way of Things

DID YOU KNOW?

By way of illustration to help us grasp what the Preacher means by trying to learn "everything," I think of a concept in the Taoist religion. Taoism is a false religion built around Eastern mysticism, but it has a shadow of truth in its concept of the tao (pronounced "dow"). The basic meaning of the Chinese word is "way," as in a road or a path. Everything living has its tao, and to truly understand anything one must learn its way. For example, learning the tao of an eagle is to know why it does what it does and what function it serves within the rest of nature. Every tao together constitutes the one great tao that is the way of absolute truth.

I might say that Solomon sought the Tao te Ching, the Way of [absolute] Truth, by trying to learn the tao of everything in creation. He found it futile for reasons we will see. Taoism claims that truth comes through mysticism—meditation, inner enlightenment, and so forth. This mysticism is merely a resignation to the fact that the Preacher reveals. Frustrated with the inability of the mind to find ultimate truth rationally, the mystic tries the opposite, shutting down his mind in a vain hope that this somehow brings truth. To use the image of Ecclesiastes, this is as useless as trying to catch the wind by lying down and falling asleep.

His point about learning is that, as with all other labors (remember his theme), there is no end to it. You can study and memorize and master day by day, year after year, for your whole life, and still have only the first grain of sand from a beach of potential knowledge. To switch images, there is an ocean of knowledge out there but we all have pint-sized brains. Learning for its own sake is not wrong, but it is not in itself a means of lasting accomplishment or permanent satisfaction. Seeking fulfillment in education is like chasing wind.

The obvious solution to the search for something of lasting value was wisdom and knowledge. So much for that! Even though God was pleased when young King Solomon requested wisdom above all else, wisdom did not give true satisfaction.

Wisdom is not a bad thing. It is a very good thing when used in God's will. But wisdom was not the solution to the Preacher's quest. Remember that we have barely started the book, so don't jump to any conclusions yet. Please take in everything this part of God's Word has to say before you make any extreme conclusions, such as dropping out of school because the Bible supposedly says that learning is a puff of air.

Seeking Fulfillment through Amusement

2:1-3 Read 2:1-3 to pick up with the next phase of the great search for satisfaction. If musing didn't do it, maybe the opposite pursuit will—amusement, which means "not thinking." The Preacher talks to himself again and decides to try living it up. It may be, he thinks, that the pursuit of pleasure will provide permanent satisfaction for his inner desire. But very quickly he finds it empty; verse 2 records his conclusions about laughter and mirth (mirth is the elated feeling of being very happy or amused). He follows the same line into verse 3, trying some chemical stimulation in the form of wine. Unlike many, he kept his wisdom even in the midst of revelry.

Pause to consider the capacity this man had to pursue pleasure. He was an absolute monarch, incredibly wealthy, highly esteemed around his part of the world. There was no practical limit to the amount of amusement he could afford to indulge in.

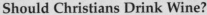

Now, I have known or heard of lots of people who look for escapes in these sorts of amusements. Stand-up comics and comedy TV and movies constitute the only pleasure some people have. Others rest their daily hopes on wine (or beer or liquor or various drugs) and drench their sorrows into oblivion every weekend, if not every evening. The Preacher

---

Should Christians Drink Wine?

Matters of testimony and evil associations in modern American culture make it generally impossible for a Christian today to drink alcohol even in moderation without sinning. While drinking wine is not in itself a sin (Gen. 27:28; Num. 6:20; John 2), drunkenness (Prov. 23:30-31) and identification with worldliness (I John 2:15) are sins. There is no medical reason for a Christian today in America to drink.

25

tells us he went there, and he tried all that, and declares that all of it is vapor.

Seeking Fulfillment through Accomplishments

2:4 Well, that wasn't the answer either, so next he tries personal accomplishment. Thinks the Preacher, "If satisfaction does not come from what I do to myself, whether I amass knowledge or indulge in laughter, then maybe it will come from what I do in the world around me." Thus he sets to work building things.

Once again, his status allowed him to pursue his goal to a greater extent than you or I ever will. He had the resources of an entire nation, a nation mightily blessed by God. The architectural wonders of Solomonic Jerusalem are only hinted at in Scripture, but they are still legendary. First Kings 7:1 records that it took thirteen years to build Solomon's palace in Jerusalem. He also built a separate house for the daughter of Pharaoh, his first queen. Archaeology has informed us that Solomon had lesser palaces in his fortress towns Hazor, Megiddo, and Gezer. He practically doubled the size of Jerusalem. He built "The House of the Forest of Lebanon," a marvelous building of cedar pillars and trimmings. First Kings 10 describes Solomon's shipping endeavors and his opulent gold and ivory throne.

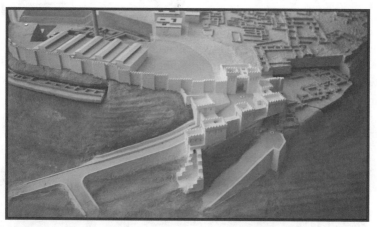

In the museum at Megiddo is a model of ancient Megiddo, showing the Solomonic gate. Solomon extensively rebuilt Megiddo and several other Israelite cities.

:5-6 If you have ever seen a large botanical garden, you have an idea of what the king constructed. Records of ancient hydrologic works amaze us even today. The king was able to enjoy the sense of fulfillment that comes with envisioning, designing, and erecting great structures. Imagine that you are an architect. You have the means to combine the aesthetically wondrous with the functionally sound into a perfect blend of science and art. People from all around the world come to see your masterpiece, gazing in awe and walking all through it. Scholars and students study it to learn principles of design. And it is not only for display; it is the most elegant and efficient office building in the world, a status symbol to the corporation headquartered inside its walls.

When you are finished with this wonder, you build another, this time a great hospital. Then you build a massive football stadium that looks as delicate as a rose. You build national monuments, museums, libraries, state parks, and on and on. The Preacher had both the mind and the means to do all this in his day, and he did it. But did it provide the permanent satisfaction he sought?

Seeking Fulfillment through Possessions

:7 Going beyond personal accomplishment, Solomon sought satisfaction in accumulated possessions. He gathered servants, cattle, and money. Human servants were "bond servants," effectively owned by their master, though (in Israel) protected by the same civil law as everyone else. We need a word less emotionally charged than *slave* but more forceful than *servant* to get across what these people were. "Bondslave" is sometimes used, but doesn't mean anything to most of us unless it is defined. But the point is that servants were a major sign of wealth. Slaves were very expensive. Purchasing a servant meant paying for all the future work he would do. Humans live longer and can do more varied and complicated kinds of work than any animal or machine. Imagine we teleport slave economics from the ancient world to our modern world. To buy a 20-year-old servant is to pay for the work of a literate man of average intelligence who, as a standard laborer, would earn roughly 30 thousand dollars a year for the next fifty years.

Sufficient to say, this man was rich even for a king. Verse 8 shows that he collected fine treasures in addition to sheer bulk commodities. He gathered the special treasures, such as ivory, jewels, and rare woods. He bought expensive artifacts from many foreign lands. He loved music, too, and brought male and female singers to Jerusalem to entertain him and enrich his mind and emotions. No one is positive what the last two words of verse 8 mean. Suggestions range from "musical instruments" (which makes sense in the context because singers were just mentioned) to "many concubines" (which makes sense when we remember how Solomon went crazy with women, acquiring some 1000 wives and concubines over his forty-year reign). Either way, it is a sign of Solomon's extraordinary wealth and prosperity.

I think it most likely that "many concubines" is the correct reading. This was not moral or wise. Solomon's numerous foreign women turned his heart away from the Lord. God's will for marriage was clear from Genesis 2 forward—one man and one woman for life. But Solomon followed the failings of pagan kings in amassing women as treaty guarantees, status symbols, and objects of pleasure. This same thinking is echoed today by men whose claim to fame is the number of women they have "conquered." The Preacher tried that path, too, and found that it did not offer what he had hoped. It was never enough; he always craved more, and the more he got the less satisfied he was. Later in Ecclesiastes, the Preacher will return to the subject of marriage and give us his retrospective counsel.

:9-10 These two verses summarize the king's search for fulfillment through personal accomplishment. Even through all his aggrandizement, the wisdom God had given him remained. By it he was able to understand the ultimate fruitlessness of all he attempted. He thoroughly enjoyed his indulgent quest, as you might expect. But I am curious to know how much he sinned during his search for satisfaction.

:11 He did take great pleasure and gained a limited sense of fulfillment in his achievements, accomplishments, and indulgences. He calls his portion the joy he received from his manifold labors. But then, in verse 11, he steps back and looks at what must have been years of his life gone by, and declares that all of it was vapor and chasing wind. The joy he reaped was his *portion*, but there was no *profit*. No profit under the sun, anyway.

Conclusions

:12 Having finished his search, the Preacher turns back to reflect on his discoveries. He repeats the expression "wisdom and madness and folly" that stands as a figure of speech for everything. He observes that the king, meaning himself, had done as much as anyone ever would be able to do to explore the meaning of all things. Therefore, he implies, I should listen to his conclusions because I will never know as well as he does what happens when you really live it up. Admittedly, I will never have anywhere near the amount of wisdom, knowledge, wealth, possessions, laughter, pleasure, accomplishment, and fame that King Solomon had. Neither will you, or anyone you know.

This is the first observation, given in two parts: wisdom is as much better than foolishness as it possibly can be, but despite this fact, the same fate ultimately overtakes the wise man as the fool. Naturally enough he wonders why he became wise and concludes that even wisdom is vapor. The wise man is vapor. He was better than the fool, to be sure, but both die and both are forgotten by following generations.

:17 If I were to search high and low for satisfying good and exhaust every resource of human life in my search, yet find it all in vain, how would I feel about life? Remember that "hate" means *to reject* in Hebrew. The emotional element is there, but it is to be expected when I consider the involvement of this man in his search for fulfillment. I am not surprised he was frustrated at this point. I am not surprised he "hates life," or rejects it as the solution to his search. Despite the joy and satisfaction he took in all his endeavors, all of it was vapor and chasing wind. Everything under the sun was transitory; all his works were fleeting, and the pleasure he took from them evaporated like steam.

:18-23 The Preacher reiterates his conclusion that life under the sun is not the place to find satisfaction. At this point in his argument, I might be depressed. I expect that at this moment in the life he is recounting, Solomon was indeed depressed, but I am only in Chapter 2, so I will hear him out.

I cannot dispute what he says, anyway. Read through verses 18-20, and see if it isn't the truth. All the great works Solomon did remained when he was gone. They stayed where he built them, under the sun; when Solomon died he went beyond the sun, taking nothing with him. This teaching flew in the face of contemporary beliefs. Have you studied ancient Egypt? The Pharaohs were buried with their vast possessions, apparently supposing that they would be able to enjoy them eternally in the  next life. Yet, when archaeologists excavated their tombs three and four thousand years later, they found that, unless thieves had broken in and stolen the goods, they were still there! And most importantly, Pharaoh was not there. There were a few mummies, of course, but no matter how skillful the embalming, the result is still just a rotted corpse, not a human being. King Tut is gone, but his gold is in a museum. He did not gain one day of enjoyment from his possessions after he died. King Solomon's God-given wisdom taught him this fact before his death, but nothing he could do could change it. No wonder he paused to ponder why he had engaged in great works. Did he waste his life?

His main point about laboring under the sun is that it is definitely not the source of ultimate meaning or permanent satisfaction. Hard work and sacrifice bring nothing that lasts. This is divine wisdom. It is God's revealed Word, and it is unarguable. All the energy expended in the world around you is devoted to impermanent goals. The rich get richer, but so what—they still die, and the pleasure of wealth is forever gone. Celebrities and professional athletes bask in the limelight for a few years and then fade into history, remembered for a generation or so at best because of a few achievements that mean nothing in God's eyes. Great learning and wisdom win applause and respect, but they don't satisfy in themselves, and scholars die just like fools and criminals do.

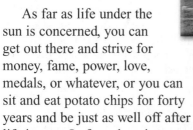

As far as life under the sun is concerned, you can get out there and strive for money, fame, power, love, medals, or whatever, or you can sit and eat potato chips for forty years and be just as well off after life is over. In fact, devoting yourself to a temporal goal earns a lot more pain and exhaustion than sprawling on the couch and eating chips. This is the sad truth for most people who labor in the fallen, sinful world around you. But the question that cries out of my own heart is, Does it have to be this way?

Why It All Fails

:24-26 The Preacher comes to the end of his first main section with a preliminary admonition that is stated with such startling simplicity that it is easy to miss. For the first time, Solomon says plainly what God has done. God has given as a gift to man the routine of eating and drinking and enjoying his labor. This does not alter the fact that all is vapor; rather, it begins to reveal *why* life is vapor and what we are supposed to do with it. *The regular enjoyable things in life, like eating and drinking and working, were never intended to provide permanent satisfaction.*

I have to understand verse 25 very clearly in order to grasp the Preacher's point in this section. It is a rhetorical question that

In Solomon's Steps?

Think About It!

It is natural to wonder whether young people ought to follow Solomon's example in devoting themselves to sensual pleasures. Other parts of Scripture, some of which Solomon wrote, deal directly with sins of excess. There is no doubt that Solomon did not want young people doing as he had done.

In Proverbs (5:15-23), later in Ecclesiastes (9:9), and in the Song of Solomon, King Solomon counsels monogamy. Even though he was not monogamous himself, he urges young men to cling to one wife. Many Old Testament incidents illustrate the damage of polygamy, even when God tolerated it (Gen. 16 and 30-31). Proverbs 20:1 and 23:29-35 warn against the sin of getting drunk with wine. Drunkenness violates the explicit word of God.

In Ecclesiastes 2, Solomon is not condoning these things but giving a good reason to avoid them: they are vapor. They offer contentment but fail to provide it. Solomon indulged himself, he says, and was left hollow and disillusioned until he looked to God alone for satisfaction. He wants to spare young people from repeating his mistake by teaching them to satisfy themselves with God for their whole lives.

The so-called Epicurean refrains teach that, once we look to God as the real source of fulfillment, we realize that life's transitory pleasures are His gift to us to enjoy in measure until we join Him in eternity. In effect, Solomon is giving his "testimony" of how God showed him the emptiness of his former sinful ways and led him to abandon them for something infinitely better.

---

reads, "Who can eat or enjoy anything without Him?" Some misunderstandings have arisen due to a textual variant; that is, some Hebrew Bible manuscripts have *me* as the last word instead of *Him*. It isn't disastrous to the meaning, but it makes little sense for Solomon to refer to himself here. He is talking about God's giving of life's pleasures as a gift, so "without Him" is much more likely. The difference between *me* and *him* in Hebrew is less than the difference between hand-written lower case *l* and *i* in English. You can see how a small misreading could appear. But the "Him" is very likely what Solomon originally wrote.

Don't miss the power of this verse; the rhetorical question implies the answer "No one." No one can enjoy any good apart from God! All the things King Solomon explored came up short of providing permanent satisfaction; but looking back he realizes that God is the one who made it this way. God doesn't want man to find fulfillment in pleasure. He gave pleasure as a gift to be enjoyed in measure. Those who toil for vapor are serving only to provide more goods to those whom God has given the ability to truly enjoy life—His children. Properly enjoying life demands seeing it from the right perspective, and that is God's perspective.

Review and Discussion

1. Suppose someone tells you that Ecclesiastes was probably written by King Hezekiah, who ruled the southern kingdom of Judah from about 716 to 686 B.C. (200+ years after Solomon). How should you respond, according to the material in this chapter? Summarize the evidence for your position.

2. Suppose someone else tells you that Ecclesiastes is most likely the work of a Jewish scholar from the Intertestamental Period (approx. 100 B.C.) who had embraced Epicurean philosophy and was trying to make the Jews see that the worship of God was compatible with Epicureanism. How should you respond, according to the information in this chapter?

3. Imagine you are a math teacher, happily loading your students down with homework. One of them, named Ingamar, objects that the Bible says that there is no good reason to learn math. When you ask to see where, she points out Ecclesiastes 1:18. According to this chapter, how would you explain to Ingamar the meaning of that verse as it relates to math homework?

4. Suppose you meet a Christian who has decided that eating anything but vegetables and water is wrong because it indulges his body instead of developing his spirit. First, what does Ecclesiastes say about such a conviction? Second, *should* you confront this person with what Ecclesiastes says?

5. Suppose you meet a man at work who is really living for pleasure: he works a good job but has no family and spends every dime on weekend fun. One day he comes to you and confides that he isn't all that happy, and wonders what he is missing in life. Based on Ecclesiastes, what should you say to him concerning his lifestyle?

Overview

Introduction: Theme is stated—all is vapor. 1:1-3

Illustration: Nature endlessly repeats its actions. 1:4-11

The king's quest for fulfillment is reported. 1:12–2:16

The king expresses frustration at the failures of life to satisfy, and rejects life as the source of satisfaction. 2:17-23

Solution: God has given the good things in earthly life for our temporary enjoyment, not for our permanent fulfillment. 2:24-26

(first Epicurean refrain—2:24)

CHAPTER THREE

A Heart for Eternity

3

Memory Verse: Ecclesiastes 3:11

:1-8 The third chapter opens with a new declaration. As a reader, my question is whether this declaration continues the theme of section 1 (Chapters 1-2) or begins a new line of thought that develops the Preacher's message in a new way. Read his declaration in v. 1, and then read the poem with which he expands it. After you read through fourteen pairs of "polar opposites," what impression do you get? How would you re-state the poem in a single sentence? After reading it I think it sounds as if there is a time for *everything.* Indeed, that is the Preacher's point. His poem beautifully expresses what he wrote in v. 1—every event on earth has its appointed time. By writing a poem about it, he makes the fact more striking and memorable. Obviously, it is important for me to understand that there is an appointed time for everything. But where he is going with this?

:9-10 The next two verses (v. 9-10) echo the latter part of Chapter 2, so I know we are building on the theme, "All is vapor." There is no remainder or leftover to a laborer after all his labor, but God gave man that labor. When I put this thought together with the times poem, I get this: though life under the sun seems to be full of ceaseless repetition without any permanent fruit, God has appointed every event to occur in its appropriate time and does not intend for this life to carry over into the next life.

:11 Now comes what many people consider the key paragraph to the book of Ecclesiastes.

Verses 9 and 10 actually begin it, so read from there down through verse 14. Think carefully about the significance of verse 11. God is the one who is responsible for making everything appropriate in the proper time. All of the manifold events, like those in the times poem, happen when they ought to. In other words, the transience and repetition that the Preacher perceives are not tragic necessity; God purposefully ordains them to accomplish His goals and serve our good.

The next statement of verse 11 may be the Preacher's most enlightening. He continues the thought from the previous sentence and couples with it a vital piece of information. The word translated "world" or "eternity" means *indefiniteness*. It may not necessarily be infinity, but it is an unlimited amount from the user's viewpoint. God has set "indefiniteness" in the heart (the mind; the soul or inner man) of man. This means that the void inside you that cannot be finally satiated by any level of pleasure or achievement is there because God put it there.

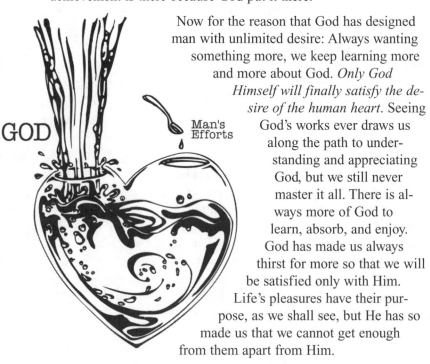

GOD

Man's
Efforts

Now for the reason that God has designed man with unlimited desire: Always wanting something more, we keep learning more and more about God. *Only God Himself will finally satisfy the desire of the human heart.* Seeing God's works ever draws us along the path to understanding and appreciating God, but we still never master it all. There is always more of God to learn, absorb, and enjoy. God has made us always thirst for more so that we will be satisfied only with Him. Life's pleasures have their purpose, as we shall see, but He has so made us that we cannot get enough from them apart from Him.

This means that all those things King Solomon tried and found hollow, the same things that so many people look to for satisfaction, serve to show us how much we need God. Many of these things are not wrong, but they serve a purpose other than giving us permanent satisfaction. All knowledge building, wisdom winning, personal attainment, and grandiose achievement can further our growth in God's likeness because they are all imitations of God. To explain, God made us in His image, meaning essentially that we can have dominion over creation and be morally righteous. But we are not born just like Him. We first have to repent of sin and be converted to righteousness. Then we progressively grow more like God by learning about Him, obeying Him more diligently, and literally getting to know Him. Acting like Him, in our little ways, makes us more like Him.

Nearly every desire that Solomon over-indulged, you can meet within legitimate, God-honoring bounds. When you do, each desire can make you a little more like God. You never become God when you learn, gain a new skill, make something, and so forth, but you do become more of what a human being in God's image ought to be. Even being joyful is being like God, for He is perfectly and eternally joyful. He has other emotions, including fierce anger and deep sorrow, but these do not disturb His deep-seated joy.

However constructive the pursuit of your desires may be, it is 1) worthless unless done for God and in His way and 2) even then ultimately unable to fill up the hole in your heart. You have to have God Himself. To borrow an old saying, there is a hole in every human heart. The shape of that hole is infinite in all respects. The hole is thus a God-shaped hole. Only God can fill it, and only with Himself.

Choosing Joy, Doing Good, Fearing God

The next three verses make three statements that build on verse 11. They teach the proper actions we should have in response to the truth revealed in v. 11, which is the primary message of Ecclesiastes. We are to rejoice, to do good, to take joy in our work, and especially to fear God.

:12 First, the Preacher is sure that the only way people can have "good" is to do two things: rejoice and do good in life. This is a continuation of 2:24, but expands the focus to volitional joy. Volitional means that you act voluntarily, or willfully; you choose to do something. We are supposed to rejoice, or be joyful, or be happy. We have plenty of reasons to be joyful, but the command does not depend on any reasons. We are to actually choose joy!

In addition, we are to "do good" during earthly life. *Good* is about as broad a word in Hebrew as it is in English. It means everything from kind deeds done to your neighbor to wholesome labor. The only way I can *have* good in this life is to be happy and *do* good.

:13 Second, enjoyment of physical pleasure and taking satisfaction in achievement is a gift of God. The Preacher has said such before (2:24), and continues the thought here. God actually must grant the ability to enjoy the vapor of life. He does not make this life permanent (for which we must be thankful) but He can make it fun and rewarding in its limited way.

:14 Third, the work of God is set in contrast to our vaporous works. Unlike ours, His work lasts forever. Man cannot reduce or enlarge it. This is a continuation of the theme of God's sovereign control. Verse 11 made a strong assertion of God's sovereignty. Now the Preacher holds up before us the unchangeable work of God; life may be a fruitless routine from our perspective, but it is not fruitless from His!

The climax of the paragraph is the last clause of verse 14, which gives the reason God has made man unable to find anything satisfying beyond Him. God wants us to fear Him. Fear is a vitally important word in the Old Testament. It means essentially living life in awareness of God. When I fear God, I am aware of God in everything I think, say, and do. I realize that He knows all about me, I know what He wants and what displeases Him. I am afraid to disobey Him but want instead to please Him in everything. This fear of God is practically equivalent to true religion and, therefore, to biblical Christianity. Notice that fear, far from excluding joy and happiness, actually requires them. The fear is not a cowering terror, like that of a dog whimpering under your bed during a thunderstorm. It is a reverential awe that is the natural and proper response to God's presence, coupled with love, praise, and worship.

AWARE OF GOD

LOVE TO PLEASE GOD

AFRAID TO DISOBEY GOD

} FEAR OF GOD

:15 Compare with 1:9-10. The Preacher picks up a theme that he started earlier—life under the sun is very repetitive. I may think I have come up with a new experience or accomplishment, but people before me, even if long forgotten, have done essentially the same thing. God examines what is past, holding us all accountable for our actions.

:16-17 The theme of injustice crops up. Under the sun, judges and rulers may be wicked and crooked even though their responsibility before God is to dispense justice. Beyond the sun, matters will be different when the one true Judge rights all wrongs. Verse 17 echoes verse 1, reiterating the assurance that God is in control of all events at all times.

:18-21 These verses give a reason that God has made man as he is. The Preacher supposes that God has tested us with unquenchable desire to demonstrate our mortality. This is true of both the righteous and the wicked, but the righteous (like the Preacher) can see beyond it. To the unregenerate man under the

Who Knows?

Think About It!

In isolation, verses 20 and 21 seem to say that there is no afterlife. But they cannot be taken in isolation for three reasons: first, ancient peoples assumed an afterlife; second, Solomon wrote Ecclesiastes under the Holy Spirit's inspiration with the rest of Scripture as background; third, elsewhere in Ecclesiastes Solomon implies that there is an afterlife (such as 8:12-13, 12:7).

Why then are these verses worded as they are? The passage as a whole, from verse 17 through verse 22, shows that Solomon's point is to prove human mortality. No one can deny the fact that we are all going to die. Verse 21, thoughtfully contemplated, sparks in the reader's mind the awareness that his eyes cannot support what was commonly assumed—that human spirits went upward while animal spirits went down (to return to earth, not to some sort of animal afterlife).

For the ungodly man, his inability to satisfy his natural desires is designed by God to show him that he is in a sense no different from an animal (v. 18). He is material, he is frail, he is little but animate dust. But whoever receives and understands the Preacher's revelation, that God has made sinful man as he is for the best of purposes, realizes that his mortality is a relief from the burdens of this life, like injustice (v. 16), and a release from its concerns, allowing him happiness (v. 22).

sun, evidence of his own mortality is distasteful, often offensive, but it is truth. However, the realization that he will die can be the opening window that sheds light on his sinful, helpless condition and points him toward the Savior.

Do not think that this section denies the afterlife. It is designed to confront man with his helplessness ("that they might see that they themselves are beasts"). The passage presents man as helpless by explaining that without divine revelation, he cannot know there is an afterlife ("who knoweth . . ."). It also presents man's helplessness by showing man's inevitable death, which is essentially no different than a beast's. Those who believe in an afterlife but reject the Bible put their faith in pure imagination; if they would open their eyes, they would see people dying like animals every day.

Life is a vapor. I breathe today, but tomorrow I could return to the dust I came from and very few people would know. Fewer still would care. The human race would continue along its course, my coworkers would mourn but carry on, and even my family would eventually adapt and continue their lives. This is true whether I am a Christian or not. The difference is that, as a Christian, I know where my spirit will go and why it will go there. Everyone on earth needs to understand what God's Word says on this point. Our mortality extinguishes our groundless human pride and turns our hearts toward God.

:22 Verse 22 makes a very happy application from the foregoing section about mortality. Those who do not know God are disturbed when they frankly contemplate death, but to God's children death is liberating. There is no reason to concern oneself with the fact of death. Instead, enjoy the life God gives one day at a time and be content that you will one day die and leave this life of vapor. The hardship and sorrow that go on after you, which could be another cause of anxiety, you will never see.

Unjust Still

4:1-3 This next section opens with a resumption of the theme of injustice (from 3:16-17). Solomon is more severe this time, deciding that it is better to be dead than alive, and better yet never to be born. This is another of the statements that gets Ecclesiastes its poor reputation. But we must understand the point of view taken and the context as a whole. First, be conscious of the cyclical nature of the book as discussed earlier. The Preacher brought up this theme and offered an explanation of why the wise man does not get demoralized over injustice—God will bring perfect justice in due time (3:17). In the opening of this entirely new section, the Preacher continues the same theme to add new information to both the problem and its solution. He has not changed his mind, nor become discouraged, or been beset with senility and forgotten what he wrote earlier. It is the design of his essay.

And what he writes is just as true. Under the sun, from the human vantage point, it *is* better to be dead than to depend on corrupt human beings for justice and fairness. The living suffer. The dead have

Is Everything Due to Envy?

Think About It!

Out of context, 4:4 could seem to say that envy or rivalry motivates even Christians' works. Solomon may be using hyperbole, a sweeping statement that communicates an idea as if it were absolute for the sake of effect. We cannot apply hyperbole to a pedantic extreme. For example, if your teacher were to say, "teenagers are magnificent!" it would be unwise to assume that he would call every last individual teenager in the world "magnificent." Rather, he means that teens in general are magnificent, though there may be exceptions. He is not lying; he is using hyperbole.

The two words in verse 4:4 preceded by "all" or "every" may shed further light on exactly what the Preacher meant by this sentence. The first word means labor or toil, and the second word means success or profit. Solomon is probably saying that, out there in the work-a-day world, all of the hard work that people do to generate products and progress, they do for the sake of envy and rivalry. Hopefully, this isn't true of God's people, but in the world at large it is sadly undeniable. You could quote this verse to almost any ordinary white- or blue-collar worker, and he would heartily agree. The productivity of the business world is driven mainly by envy, not a desire to help and serve others.

As a Christian, you must live under the sun for a while, but you do not have to be blinded and enslaved by sin as so many people are. You do not have to have envy or greed driving your work; in fact, you should not. Work can and ought to be a joyful, liberating means of serving others and growing closer to God.

---

escaped (it appears), but suffered plenty in life. Only the unborn never suffered. All this is true even of God's people, as far as it goes. Eternity and heaven are not in question.

:4-6 This is another old theme resumed; labor is vapor. The new observation is that most work is motivated by envy and jealousy, the "keeping up with the Joneses" mentality. Lest you think laziness is the answer, the lazy man is a fool who destroys himself. Therefore work is good, but workers work with the wrong motives and goal in mind and so turn work into a rat race full of strife and tension, driving themselves to an early grave. In this light, it is no wonder that rest is better than wrong-headed, exhausting labor.

:7-8 The Preacher continues with more harsh realities of life under the sun. A natural question to raise is "Isn't our labor justified if we use it to benefit others?" It makes sense that work for others' sake is good. Of course, he already answered that one way, by observing that people you help may turn out to be unworthy of helping (2:18-20). Now he answers a different way; indeed it is good to help loved ones with your labor, but there are men who work themselves to death with

no one to profit by it. These are the Ebenezer Scrooges of real life, whose money profits no one, not even themselves, because they are too busy earning more to enjoy what they have.

:9-12 In contrast, it is much better to have companions. It is terrible to go through life alone. Verse 9 is not a reference to a married couple, though it certainly applies to marriage. To illustrate, the Preacher gives us three situations in which having a friend saves one from danger. Two friends are even better.

:13-16 Though it is difficult to follow the line of thought and see the connections between ideas through these middle chapters, we can follow the thematic relationships easily enough. Solomon has dealt before with the theme of kingship and its limitations (2:12, 18). He returns to it in this four-verse narrative about a boy who rises unexpectedly to become king. We don't know if Solomon was thinking of a real incident or made up a sort of parable, but his point is that, under the sun, even when true nobility gets its reward, the reward is disappointingly short-lived.

The old king goes, and that is good. A boy, humble but wise, takes the throne. By implication, he is a good king. The people throng to him appreciatively. But in time he is the old king and, even if he is always far superior to his predecessor, the next generation of his people does not appreciate him. They did not know the earlier fool of a king and don't remember how bad it was. They see today's problems and blame the present king. All of his earlier laud is gone like a vapor. Striving to find a leader who will permanently content any group of people is like chasing wind.

We need to remember this when we criticize leaders, whether in government, church, business, or wherever. No one will be the right leader indefinitely. You really cannot please all of the people all of the time, not in this fallen world under the sun. Former times were not necessarily better. People's memories are slower to remember what has improved than they are to complain about present problems. It is easy to be discontent as a follower and frustrated as a leader. All of this is vapor. Do not sweat it if people are difficult. Do the best you can, and rest assured that God will eventually blow it all away and make everything function smoothly forever.

Review and Discussion

1. Your ten-year-old brother asks about the times poem in Ecclesiastes 3, which he came across in his Bible reading. How would you explain to him, simply but clearly, what the poem means and how it applies to his Christian life?

2. How does fulfilling natural human desires make us "more like God"? How do we know where to draw the line in order to avoid sinning?

3. Why does the Preacher say that men die like animals die? What does he mean and what does he not mean by this observation?

4. Your friend has a hard time trusting God with problems because there is so much pain, sorrow, and injustice in the world. What could you say to help her, based on God's Word in Ecclesiastes?

5. Is it good for a Christian to work to help others with material things? Why or why not?

Overview

Times Poem: God arranges everything as it should be. 3:1-8

An overview of subthemes from the whole book follows the key verse. 3:12-21

Key verse: why life is like it is 3:11

Beginning of development of subthemes

Wise living in a fallen world in light of the fact that this world is not ultimate reality, but God is 4:1-16

Injustice is discouraging. 4:1-3

Labor is frustrating. 4:4-6

Wealth is inadequate. 4:7-8

Wisdom is paramount—Making friends is more important than wealth or labor. 4:9-12

Wisdom is inadequate due to human failure—humans don't appreciate wisdom. 4:13-16

CHAPTER FOUR

Oaths and Tragedies

4

Memory Verses: Ecclesiastes 5:6-7

The Preacher is in the middle of his book, between the declaration of his message and the conclusion to all of his arguments. At this point, he is developing various subthemes introduced earlier and dealing with possible objections to the idea that, although all of life is vapor, God is fully in control and will provide ultimate satisfaction to those who fear Him. These are wisdom statements that teach us how to live joyfully and live aware of God.

5:1-7 The first seven verses form a unit that emphasizes the need to fear God. The Preacher provides details on how to fear God in daily life. It is one thing to consent mentally to living my life aware of God's presence, but it is another to manifest that awareness in my day-to-day business. The ability to live life as God wants is the highest form of wisdom.

Seasoned Speech

Ecclesiastes 5:1-7 is concerned specifically with the matter of speech. Much of the evil and sorrow under the sun arises from wicked speech. The old saying, "sticks and stones may break my bones but words will never hurt me" is nonsense. Words hurt badly. In the New Testament, James probably had Ecclesiastes 5:1-7 in mind when he wrote that the tongue is a fire and that whoever can control it can control himself in every other area (James 3:1-12).

First, take special care to behave in the house of God. To King Solomon, this was the temple, the place of God's manifest presence. Today, the Church is the temple of God and the bodies of Christians are the temple of the Holy Spirit (I Cor. 3:16; 6:19). Solomon's warning certainly applies to our church buildings, but the presence of God is with us any time we meet together to worship God. Therefore, show your fear of God by being very careful with what you say around other Christians. Not only do they hear you, but God Himself hears. As the Preacher says, this is a strong reason to measure and restrain your words.

The thrust of his application is this: Do not be quick to make a vow. Modern Christians have no special "formula" for a vow (Matthew 5:37). Instead, we have the steep responsibility of having everything we say considered binding. This does not mean you cannot tell a joke or be ironic; God knows your thoughts and knows when you do not intend for anyone to take your words seriously. But when you do mean what you say, God takes it very seriously.

A vow was a promise to God to give or do something that was believed to be in line with His will. Solomon's people might give money, or animals to sacrifice, or even their children to God's service. You and I can give of our wealth, time, and so forth to God's service. God desires certain sacrifices from you, as He will reveal through prayer and His word. When you desire to give to God, it is good to make the promise, but do not fail to deliver what you promise. Do not make a decision at a camp or church service that you are not able and determined to keep—better not to make the vow at all.

Bigger Fish in the Sea

:8-9 These two verses go together, but the former is much easier to understand. The Preacher has visited the theme of injustice a couple of times before (3:16-17; 4:1-3). Here, he makes a succinct statement of encouragement. Just as everything passes away in due time, so does injustice. You may know or hear of an unjust judge, mayor, or governor, but don't worry. There is always another official higher up that will eventually call the evildoer into account, even if for his own selfish reasons. Ultimately, God is in overall control.

Verse 9 says something about a king, as you might expect since verse 8 is about bureaucracy. It is not clear exactly what the verse means, but it probably indicates the importance of a king's knowing what his people's lives are like, making him more humble and understanding.

To review, remember that the theme of injustice arises because it is a major objection to the Bible-based view of God. If God is all-knowing, all-powerful, and all-good, why do men get away with so much evil? One of the Preacher's several points concerning this question appears here: God set up human government for the purpose of punishing evildoers. It is the fault of officials when justice fails. But, in general, the wicked are restrained or punished by the government.

Moneywise

:10-12 Now the Preacher returns to his most familiar theme, the transience of earthly things. Silver was the routine currency, so this is someone who loves money. Money and the wealth it buys are vapor.

This is a good place to review the fact that Ecclesiastes often provides a balancing view to other parts of Scripture. This is not to say that any passage is only a half-truth. All are completely true in and of themselves. However, fallible human beings tend to take an interpretation of truth farther than truth really goes, entering error.

The Bible teaches private ownership of property (Exodus 20:15), the importance of labor (II Thess. 3:10), and the potential good one can do with wealth (King David is an example, as well as Barnabas and Lydia). There is nothing untrue about the Bible's teaching at any point. But people, who are corrupt by nature, may see these passages and decide that money has inherent goodness. They conclude that they should prioritize making all the money they can. Some even equate wealth with godliness. The Jews of Jesus' day made this dangerous mistake, as is evident from the disciples' surprise that rich people were less likely to be in heaven (Matt. 19:23-25). The Preacher, a great king who knew all there is to know about wealth, gives this warning: money is not satisfying. No amount will buy enough to satiate the infinite desire of a human soul.

40 English monarchs have died since William the Conqueror, but their treasures reamain on earth.

:11 Verse 11 observes that the accumulation of goods attracts only more consumers, who use up the goods and generate a need for more. We can see this in the industrialized nations of the

Think About It!

American billionaire Howard Hughes is a classic example of a man whose seemingly successful life brought him no true joy. In their biography *Howard Hughes: The Untold Story* journalists Peter Harry Brown and Pat H. Broeske complete his life's story in a final chapter entitled "Evil Under the Sun," an unacknowledged but unmistakable—and highly appropriate—allusion to the book of Ecclesiastes. Hughes's last six weeks were spent in a suite in Acapulco. The windows were sealed shut and sound proofed, making the room dark and quiet. The 70-year-old Hughes weighed only 93 pounds, suffering from dehydration, malnutrition, and syphilis. He died within days. Though everyone in America knew his name, only a handful of family—most of whom did not know him—attended his funeral.

Peter Harry Brown and Pat H. Broeske, *Howard Hughes: The Untold Story*. (New York: Dutton, 1996.)

world. The more that is produced and made available, the more people's desires extend beyond to new things. Modern economics have made more goods available to more people than ever before, but you do not see widespread satisfaction following. "Poor" countries want "rich" countries to share their capital, but are never satisfied with what they get. Rich countries, for their part, are not content to be the best off but always want more. They are not inclined to give money away.

None of this means that making money is wrong in itself. Rather, this is the Holy Spirit's universal warning about setting money up as the source of ultimate fulfillment. It is a way of thinking. We tend to either go to a materialistic extreme, looking to wealth as a god, or we go to an ascetic extreme, eschewing possessions as evil and considering poverty a spiritual asset. Neither position is true.

:12 The Preacher finishes his point with a vivid illustration. A man who works hard to earn money and take care of himself and his family will be at peace. No mention occurs of the laboring man's morals or station in life. Whatever they are, this statement remains true; routine labor brings routine satisfaction—not permanent satisfaction, of course, but the temporary kind that allows me a good night's sleep without any worries keeping me awake. My share of mental and physical energy is properly spent. I am tired, like I should be, and can enjoy God's gift of sleep. Like so much of Ecclesiastes, this principle applies to all people, not just Christians.

In contrast, a rich man (one who does not have to work for his living) is actually in a worse condition than the laborer. As a rich man, I might not have to work, but in the long run I will be unhappy and unsatisfied because of it. I may have enough money for a big meal and a good show, but I will lie awake that night restless, probably worrying over things I cannot change.

We can see here a major subpoint in the Preacher's argument. All of us need to understand something about work: it is God's gift to us. God gives only good gifts. Labor itself is not a curse, but a blessing. We are happier and healthier when we work. Sin keeps work from being enjoyable. Work provides regular, temporary satisfaction of our limitless desire. It gives us a little way to be like God, who is a tireless worker (John 5:17). It gives us a way to do good to others, providing for needs, contributing to society. God has given us work to fill our time, minds, and hands so we do not go insane from the effects of sin.

Horrors

:13 The Preacher goes on with another point about the transience of earthly things. His previous point dealt with their inability to provide permanent satisfaction. This one develops their inability to continue into the next life, the life beyond the sun.

He calls it a horror, this fact he is about to mention, a horror under the sun. An appropriate word here would be *tragedy,* something sad and disastrous. Even though this normally happens to wealthy, worldly people, it is still grieving. There is no place for glee when tragedy overtakes a rich unsaved man. Tragedy can happen to Christians. He is talking about what happens under the sun, or from the worldly point of view. From God's perspective, it may be a judgment, even a gracious judgment, when a rich man loses his wealth. Perhaps that man depended too much on his money, and God needed to deprive him of it for the sake of his soul. A wealthy Christian may experience disaster as test of faith, on the other hand. Either can well be true, but the Preacher is not looking at these aspects of disaster.

The horror is, from a human perspective, universally true. Massed wealth would seem to bring greater contentment and security. Marvelously wealthy King Solomon warns that this is not true. An unforeseeable chance event can snatch it all away. If its owner rested all of his peace in the treasure, his life is ruined. He counted on a big estate to provide for his children, but suddenly all of it is gone.

Even if you can leave something behind, you certainly cannot take it with you. I was born with nothing but my body, and I will

leave with even less. I will go to my grave wearing clothes, but the clothes and the body in them will stay there decaying until the Lord returns. The real me will be else-

where, beyond the sun, in heaven with God. But what happens to all the people who have nothing but this life to hope in? Everything they toil for throughout their lifetimes stays here when they die.

When my father-in-law died, I looked at his billed cap, his thick coat, his worn work boots. He seemed to wear them all the time. They were the closest things on earth to him; if any objects were *his,* if any things were identified with him, *they* were. But he was gone, and there they were, still there, just like they had always been. It struck me that my closest possessions, like my wristwatch, my eyeglasses, and my wedding band, things that touch me every single day, will stay here under the sun when I die. Not one dollar, nor one thread, nor one book, nor any other thing will accompany me beyond the sun. The Preacher has drawn my at-

tention once again to the truth that all is vapor.

:16 The Preacher's rhetorical ques-tion demands the answer that there is *no* profit to the one who toils for wind. Notice what this means for the worldly person who has no hope in God. He honestly has no reason to work. Of course, he ought to work but, not knowing God, he has no truly legitimate reason in his own mind to work. He will ultimately come to the same end whether he labors or not. Verse 17 de-scribes the sorrow of a life of labor that has no hope for eternity with God. Work saps strength, health, and happiness when en-gaged in for the wrong reasons.

I am amazed at the difference between living life aware of God and living life unaware of Him. (Let me make it clear that life *as a whole* is lived either aware or unaware of God, but particular days from my own life effectively illustrate the contrast.) I can spend a day at work and be totally miserable, watching the clock, my mind a thousand miles away (bad news for a writer), and then be little better when I go home. I am unsettled, unfulfilled, and discontent. But another day, I center my mind on God and on the fact that He has given me not only every reason for joy but also joy itself as a gift. Realizing that my lack of joy is due

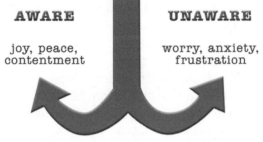

to my sin, I look at my work the way He wants me to—His gift, for my good, designed for His perfect, ultimate purposes. External circumstances are the same each day—same night's sleep, same morning routine, same wife, same breakfast, same job, same boss, same coworkers, but totally different me. It all depends on the fear, or awareness, of God.

:18 A second "Epicurean Refrain" appears in the middle of a second major section of Ecclesiastes. It is surprising at first that the application is to enjoy life, including work. Physical pleasures, even things as simple as a meal, are God's gift to make me happy while I trudge through life. Even work itself is a gift; I would be more miserable without it than with it. If I treat work the way God intends for me to, I get to enjoy it as part of my portion that makes life livable. Every man has the potential to find measured satisfaction in God's gifts. The Preacher amplifies the tragedy of going through life without enjoying it. Life is hard enough for the best people. The brevity of life under the sun is actually a mercy. Beyond the sun waits eternal life. But even in this life I can be generally very happy because God is so abundantly liberal with His gifts. I will not worry and fret over life if I take pleasure in due portion and rest my hopes in God.

Notice that God is kind even to the ungodly. Many go through life somewhat happier than they should be. Life is awful for those who are God's enemies, yet even they enjoy His gifts to the limited extent possible. Only terror waits for them beyond the sun, but as long as they are in this life, while they have time, God gives them regular foretastes of the joy they could still obtain if they looked to Him as Savior.

Back to the Beginning

6:1-2 The Preacher returns to the basic themes of life's transience and inability to offer fulfillment. Chapter 6 seems like a retelling of Chapter 2. Remember the cyclical nature of this wisdom literature. Repetition is not mere redundancy; it is reinforcement. Ecclesiastes is written to be read over and over again. Each time I read it I understand a little more and remember a little more. The themes do not stand in isolation to each other. They interlock and support one another in a grand design. That is why the cyclical pattern works so well. We have to see the themes grow together throughout the book if we are to understand them. If I read all about one theme without the others, I do not know what the Preacher's purpose is in developing that sub-theme. Reading in cycles allows them to grow together until they coalesce into a perfectly balanced whole.

Solomon's opening image is familiar from world history. Though he lived a long time after Solomon, Alexander the Great comes to mind as a classic example. Remember him, the man who conquered most of the known world while in his twenties? He had unbelievable riches, wealth, and honor, but died shortly after subjugating the massive Persian Empire. And that was that; he and his mountain of glory were eternally separated.

Alexander got his power through violence, but it was still the gift of God. All kings and nations are God's instruments. But even when a man arrives at a great estate through legitimate means, he still may lose it to another or die without enjoying it. Long life is not necessarily a guarantee that I will enjoy my wealth, either. I am amused at how big of a difference people make between dying at age 65 and dying at 85. To them, the former is a tragedy, but the latter is natural. When I hear people boast about their health, they often claim they will live to be 100. If I make it to 100, even my life insurance policy will give up and cash itself in—talk about getting great wealth without the ability to enjoy it!

:3 Yet, that is the problem: age reduces one's ability to enjoy life, and in the end he still dies. Is there really a difference in dying at 70 and dying at 90? If the extra twenty years were full of disappointments, frustrating politics, arthritis, and nursing homes, it may be better to avoid those years. Solomon is not encouraging suicide. He is making a brutally honest point that people need to face.

:4-6 The Preacher's closing illustration is gruesome, but it hits home. A miscarried child—one that is delivered prematurely and born dead—is better off than a man, even a wealthy man with a big family, who leads a long but unfulfilling life. The miscarriage never sees the sun, but the man spent his sad life under its rays. They both go to the ground in the end, only one went with years of hardship upon him. It is what lies beyond the sun that makes life worth it.

Alexander the Great

DID YOU KNOW?

Alexander's father, Philip of Macedon, conquered and united the Greeks into a single kingdom. Tutored by the great philosopher Aristotle, Alexander gained an ambition to rule the whole world. Shortly after becoming king he led his first expedition against the massive Persian empire and, through a series of brilliant campaigns, subjugated all of it. (His remarkably rapid conquest had been prophesied in Daniel's vision of the goat and ram in Daniel 8.)

Alexander would have continued into India had not his army refused to march farther east. It is said that Alexander wept because he had no more lands to conquer. He died only a few years afterward in mysterious circumstances at the age of 35. His vast empire was split into three by his followers who warred among themselves for years afterward.

:7-9 Chapter 2 is still echoing in the Preacher's words. A life of labor is unsatisfying, a wise man is ultimately no better off than a fool, and so forth. He was very down about this and the seeming discrepancies of life. Has he forgotten that? No, of course not; it is merely that cyclical process again. He is going to elaborate his point further, so he reviews these key observations the same way a chemistry teacher might review the Periodic Table's structure several times while you learn all the elements. Get this straight and do not forget it, the Preacher says: life and the desires you have are vapor, and pursuing fulfillment is chasing the wind.

:10-12 Hearkening back to the illustration with which he opened this essay, the Preacher states that there is nothing new. Everything under the sun existed before; the world moves on in seemingly ceaseless repetition. Man thinks himself to be something impressive, but he is really very limited. I do not know if the Preacher had God in mind when he wrote in verse 10 that a man cannot resist one stronger than himself. He may have meant that a human being is really quite puny and helpless, open to exploitation and enslavement by all sorts of things. But it is certainly true that God is stronger, and that no man can resist Him.

Verse 11 says that many things multiply vapor. None of these things are lasting, so there is no profit, no remainder, to a man. But most people do not realize this truth. They waste their limited years on pursuing vapor. They lead lives of vapor, as verse 12 says, also likening it to a shadow—real, but insubstantial and transient. Men do not know what follows them under the sun. They may receive honor or reproach, but they won't know it. Life under the sun goes on wholly apart from the dead.

Review and Discussion

1. From its uses in this chapter, explain the biblical meaning of the "fear of God."

2. Explain what a "wisdom section" is, such as the one in Ecclesiastes 5:1-7. Describe their function in Ecclesiastes.

3. Evaluate the following statement according to the material in this chapter:

   "Christians should never make vows."

4. Summarize the biblical view of wealth.

5. Describe the disaster that the Preacher calls a "horror."

6. Is it good to live a long life?

Overview

Wisdom is paramount, so fear God! 5:1-20

Be wise in words/fear God in your speech. 5:1-7

Oppressors should fear God. 5:8-9

Fear God in your abundance. 5:10-12

Wealth is transient, so fear God. 5:13-17

Conclusion: The solution is to enjoy good things wisely, but not to look to them as the absolute. 5:18-20 (second Epicurean refrain, 5:20)

Earthly life is transient. 6:1-12

Wealth is transient. 6:1-6

Labor and wisdom are transient. 6:7-9

Life is repetitious and transient. 6:10-12

CHAPTER FIVE

Life from the Long View

5

Memory Verses: Ecclesiastes 7:16-18

The first fourteen verses of chapter 7 are poetry. The Preacher reintroduced some basic themes in chapter 6, and now he expands on other familiar themes—the importance but impermanence of wisdom, apparent injustice in life, and his search for ultimate satisfaction. This section contains some instructions that are easy to misunderstand. They teach the importance of life's balance. Ironically, teaching about balance is difficult to keep in balance. People tend to take only one side of an argument and then go too far with it, ignoring the other side. As you study this section, take time to digest everything the Preacher says without jumping to conclusions.

Wisdom Poem

His opening poem is about wisdom. The poem builds on the praise of wisdom in 2:12-14 and echoes this style of the Book of Proverbs. Solomon accomplishes a dual purpose with the poem. First, the poem gives instructions that are in themselves good and profitable to a godly person. Second, it introduces further comments on the value of wisdom. Earlier, Solomon exalted wisdom but rejected it as the source of ultimate satisfaction. Now he elaborates the benefits of wisdom, but still finds it inadequate to provide absolute truth.

7:1 Good oil was both valuable and useful. Not petroleum, "oil"

usually meant olive oil, one of the ancient world's most important commodities. Even the lowest quality oil was good for food. Higher grades served ceremonial and cosmetic purposes. It also made good lamp fuel. In Scripture, we see oil used for anointing kings and priests. It was good manners to dump oil on an honored guest, strange as it may seem (Ps. 23:5). If you've never rubbed olive oil on your hands and face, try it sometime. Once you get over the novelty, you may see why they liked it so much.

With all that in mind, I get the point of verse 1: a good name (reputation) is really important and very satisfying. "The day of death" refers here to the legacy I leave behind, not to the relief of escaping life's hardships. Once dead, I am no longer able to tarnish my good name or soil the honor of God. Every day I live is another day I could blow it all. Now, this does not mean the Preacher wants you to pray for death; rather, it is a way of emphasizing the fact that your good name is extremely important. Notice how this contrasts his laments about the vapor of life. If it truly did not matter what we do in life, reputations would be irrelevant. But relevant they are, says the Preacher. Even though the scope of his admonition is under the sun (reputations apply only on earth—God knows the unfiltered truth), it would not mean anything without an infinite, all-just God and an afterlife. Solomon assumes I know about God and believe in the afterlife, as virtually all of his original readers did.

:2 If you want more evidence that Solomon assumes the afterlife, read verse 2. An Epicurean or a pagan hedonist would not focus on death. A philosopher who rejected the idea of an afterlife would not build up the significance of a funeral. Yet that is exactly what this verse does when it says that it is better to go to a funeral than to a party. Parties distract from real life, but a funeral reminds me of what life is—a vapor.

When I was a teenager, both of my grandfathers died within six months of each other. After the second funeral, I wanted to stay away from funeral homes forever. But that was a profitable experience because it sobered and matured me. I thought about death, and wondered how my life would look when I surveyed it in retrospect. I could look over the lives of my grandfathers and see what they had done, good and bad. I wondered, when my own grandson reviews my brief life, what will he see?

:3 It may seem hard to reconcile this statement with the Preacher's exhortations to eat and drink and enjoy life, but only if we read more into this than he says. He is not contradicting what he said earlier, but is in fact building on it. It is not wrong to enjoy pleasure; it is right. But it is better to understand the reality of life. A godly person must do both in balance. To understand pleasure, one must understand sobriety. In fact, sadness does not necessarily preclude inner joy. A mature view of life results in both sorrow over the sin and pain in life and utter, underlying assurance that God will make all things right in the end. Taken together with the "Epicurean refrains," this verse shows that enjoying life does not mean giving oneself to emotional abandon. Christians are to enjoy life God's way, but God's way does not include narcotics abuse, gluttony, or sexual perversity. Joy requires a sober, realistic outlook on life under the sun.

:4 Verse 4 reiterates verse 1 with an emphasis on the thought life. The "heart" is what we call the mind, encompassing the thoughts and will as well as emotions. A wise man thinks about his mortality and the consequent need to make every day count. A fool wants to escape from life. He thinks about the next party or the next carnival that will get his mind off life. Not that pleasure is wrong, but preoccupation with pleasure is foolish. It will not lead to joy but to constant disappointment and frustration because pleasure is never enough to satisfy. Only a fool thinks so.

Do you see the tension between this wisdom poem and other parts of the book? It points to the need for balance, which is the theme of this chapter.

:5-6 The next two verses continue to praise the wise man over the fool. Proverbs talks about the value of taking rebukes from wise men (Prov. 9:8; 13:1). "The song of fools" means their attempt to entertain and befriend you. We don't normally sing songs to each other today, but we do listen to music together. Before the electronic age, music came only from a performer. It was a sign of friendship to sing a song to someone. (I suppose it still is for those who can carry a tune.) But if the man seeking friendship was a fool, it is better to do without his friendship. Remember that a fool is not a person who is unintelligent but a person who is a rebel against God. A fool hates rebukes. But friendship with a fool can lead me into sin, while obedience to the wise leads to a joyful, God-fearing life. Thorns make an annoying crackle when they burn. The Preacher likens the noise to fools' laughter. But he calls it vapor. Great as it may be, the superiority of wisdom over folly is vapor.

:7 I am not sure if there is a connection in thought between verses 6 and 7. A thought connection means that the ideas are joined in a logical relationship, like a cause-effect sequence or a grounds-result chain. The first word of verse 7 can mean several different things, such as "for" (because) or "surely," "since," or "indeed." Therefore it may or may not indicate a close connection.

Probably it does; the fact that corruption and bribery can ruin a wise man is a sign that even wisdom is vapor.

:8 Verse 8 goes on along the same line as the rest of the wisdom poem by focusing attention on outcomes more than initiations. It may be exciting to take up a new endeavor, but what matters is what it actually accomplishes. This isn't to discourage us from taking initiatives. It is to make us consider the long-term effects of our actions and to focus on their impact. Likewise, it is better to be patient and reflective than to be hotheaded or rash. All these proverbs are contributing to the importance of the mature, reasoned, long-range perspective of life. You can develop this perspective while young, and the younger you do, the better total life you will lead.

:9-10 The next verse builds on verse 8. Verse 10 is a gemstone for young people who tire of hearing how much better things were in "the good ol' days." The next time someone starts to tell you that, you will be able to show him this verse. Of course, you also need to understand the context in which it appears. This poem is about the long-range view of life. The former days are gone and will not return. They may have been better, but longing for what cannot be is not wise. Working to bring back whatever made the old days good is wise, however. Besides, former days may not have been so much better after all, in God's all-seeing eyes. Our destination is more important than our origin.

:11-12 These two verses compare the safety/security benefits of wisdom and money. While money offers a measure of future security, wisdom preserves life. Wisdom is better than money.

:13-14 The ultimate reason to take the long view of life is the sovereignty of God. Hearkening back to the key section 3:11-15 and to 1:15, the Preacher reminds me that all of life is in God's hands. It is a great comfort to know that no one can ever change that. One objection to the idea of God's sovereignty is the fact that terrible things happen to godly people. This is a perennial problem: the Holy Spirit devoted the entire book of Job to the same problem (which was probably also written through the pen of Solomon). In Ecclesiastes, the fact that God can do anything He wants to is a reason for peace, security, and joy.

Our problem is that we don't know as much as God knows. He will send along good days, and He wants us to enjoy them. There are days when your family is getting along, you feel good, your team won, and the world generally looks rosy. Drain the good out of these days and enjoy every minute. They are God's gift. But other days will come that are not so good. Even the godliest person encounters adversity. The Preacher lets us in on a startling secret: God is the one who sends hard times as well as good times. God makes them both in their appropriate portion (remember 3:11) to this purpose, that man should find nothing beyond Him. Adversity teaches us dependence, and dependence on God is the way we should be naturally. The mature view of life recognizes that it is God who allows trials and troubles, frustration and disappointment, to display to us our dependency on Him.

Notice that the entire fourteen-verse poem draws together through the first and last verses. They put forth the proposition that life's difficult moments are really the most beneficial. Under the sun, joy is not to be dependent on circumstances. Be joyful in the good times, and be joyful in the hard times, as God intends. Since He is in sovereign control, He will work everything well in the end.

Life in Balance

:15-18 For this next section it is vital to understand the fundamental Hebrew meanings of *righteous* and *wicked*. Like most religious words, they had a mundane (ordinary) meaning that formed the basis for their use in religious contexts. *Righteous* basically describes something that is straight or "conforming to a set standard." A measuring ruler is "righteous," the ancient Hebrew could say. Weights and measures were to be righteous (Lev. 19:36; the word describing weights and measures is the Hebrew "righteous"), meaning that they had to match standards accurately. A thieving merchant might load his scales or rest his thumb unseen on the scales to cheat his customer out of money. Those

RIGHTEOUS

scales were then "wicked," not conforming to the external standard.

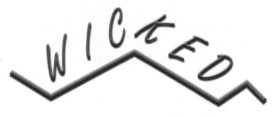

You can see why these words work so well in their religious senses, which are very close to the meanings of the English words we use to translate them, *righteous* and *wicked*. The religious sense of each word occurs far more often in the Bible than the mundane senses (naturally, since the Bible is primarily concerned with religion). We would never use those two English words in a nonmoral sense, but we have similar dual-use words like *crooked* and *pure*. *Crooked* means uneven, not straight. We can use it to mean someone is a criminal: "That man was a crooked investment manager." *Pure* means uniform, not mixed with other substances. I can say that orange juice is pure without any moral connotation (unless I consider mixed fruit juice a sin). But I can also say, "She has a pure heart," clearly a moral use of the word.

With that in mind, read these four verses, thinking of the mundane meanings of righteous and wicked. We are not looking at men who are morally upright or morally evil. These are men whose lives conform to a standard. Better words in English might be rigid and lax. A rigid, strict man who is conscientious of details, order, and keeping his life clean would seem likely to do better in life, but it isn't always so. Contrariwise, a lax man, a careless and lazy individual, whom you would expect to die young if anyone did, may live to see a long life.

It's good to be wise, but being overly wise is to be a "know-it-all." It's wrong to be a fool to any degree. A truly wise man is at neither of these unpleasant extremes; he knows much that is valuable, but remains humble, recognizing his limitations.

The standard assumed in these verses is not the law of God, but different norms of expectations, like societal or personal norms. Righteousness here means strictness in meeting expectations. Wise means skillful or capable. Do you understand what this is prohibiting? Excessive conformity to a standard, even a good standard, can ruin me. When it is a case of human standards or expectation, I must not look on them as absolute. I will wear myself out trying to be perfectly right.

To illustrate, consider society's idea of proper exercise and diet. Is it good or bad to eat right and stay in shape? It is good, so the standard has a good goal. But it is not equivalent to God's law. Attempting to live in perfect conformity to diet and exercise norms to the point of anxiety will wear a person out until it is counter-productive to health.

Likewise, do not be too lax. Sloppiness and laziness are not wise for anyone. They can send you to an early grave. To continue our illustration, completely ignoring dieting will lead to obesity, poor health, and even premature death.

The solution is to keep all things in balance. Conform, but not to the point of excess that you injure yourself or others. Relax, but not so much that you become irresponsible and negligent. Surprisingly, maintaining this balance displays fear of God—but perhaps it isn't so surprising, after all. If being excessively "right-eous," in this sense, can destroy me, then it is obviously not God's will. The Lord may well lead me to give up my life in His service, but adherence to standards that He did not set is not His service. Ruining my mental or physical health for something God does not require of me is sin. It shows that I have more fear of men than of God. And being a "little wicked" in this sense is not sin; on the contrary, *never* being "wicked" is the sin. However, being excessively non-conformist is nothing but pride or laziness. It is another way of destroying myself before God's time, which is sinful.

In life, this means that I am conscientious to deliver what society asks of me, but not to the point that I displease God. To switch from the eating illustration, I could also apply this to schoolwork. I need to give what is generally expected: dedication and hard work to make the best grades I can (and yes, I am still in school, though it has been years since it was high school). However, I must not put grades above my relationship with the Lord, my relationship with my wife, or my health (physical, emotional, and mental). To do so would be sin. Neither can I slack on my schoolwork or try to get by with less than my best. I have to strike that balance to properly please God. Of course, I know that balance is best for me, just as His will is always what is best for me.

Balance is an additional component of wisdom. Taking the long view of life, you can see why balance is so important to success in life as a whole. Burning yourself out in pursuit of a short-term goal sacrifices any long-term goal you might have achieved. This is excellent wisdom for young people.

Human Inadequacy

:19-22 Again praising wisdom, the Preacher notes that no one is perfect. Everyone sometimes speaks words they would retract, given the chance. He uses the case of a servant's cursing because it was the most difficult instance in which to be gracious. A servant owed much to his master. Cursing one's master showed severe disrespect. Besides that, it was foolish because a master could impose more severe punishment than a modern boss or teacher.

Punishing the servant was not only justified; it was very easy. Servants were not equals. Imagine you overhear your nine-year-old neighbor cursing you. Probably, you would apply some correction for his impertinence, even if no more than a threat that made his bones shake. The Preacher says that wise men will be patient and humble, recognizing their own faults.

The remainder of Chapter 7 is a lamentation of the limits of wisdom. The Preacher has added much to his explanation of life under the sun, and now he returns to a painful but necessary fact: the human race is rotten despite all of God's goodness. Under the sun, life stinks; but it is man's fault, not God's. Even wisdom does not cure the illness of sin.

It seems startling that the one thing Solomon holds up as the result of his great quest is a bad woman. But remember the way Solomon in Proverbs uses a woman as the embodiment of folly. He makes a woman the embodiment of wisdom, too, so he isn't being chauvinistic. He is being poetic, as he is here in Ecclesiastes. I don't know if the king had a particular woman in mind when he wrote this, but his goal was to convey the wickedness of the whole race. The woman is bitterer than death, but the sinner is enticed by her. He can find one good man in a thousand (a figurative expression for extreme scarcity) and no good women, either. The conclusion is that, although God made mankind right (correct, proper), men have sought many *devices*. That last word is difficult because it occurs in only one other place in the Old Testament, and there it refers to war machines, like catapults (II Chron. 26:15). Evidently it refers to the invention of evil things. Chapter 7 thus ends with a sweeping observation of human corruption.

8:1-9 It is not clear where the breaks are in the Preacher's flow of thought. The first verse of what we call Chapter 8 may actually close the preceding section. Not that it matters much, because 8:1 is another of the praises of wisdom that seem to punctuate this whole section. Wisdom statements are Solomon's way of teaching how to enjoy the life God has given us. Wisdom is skill; in this case, the skill of doing God's will. God's will is that we enjoy our vaporous life His way. Hence, Solomon instructs us on some things necessary for enjoying life.

One necessary skill is maintaining the right relationships with authority, especially governmental authority. God has placed government over us for our own good. We ought to submit to its rule because of our obedience to God. God does not sanction rebellion against a human ruler. Wise men honor the king and obey his laws. They seek to resolve problems in orderly, accepted ways, not through revolution/revolt. Even though human governments may be callous and even corrupt bureaucracies, God is still in sovereign control. He will ensure that all evildoers get their punishment beyond the sun, regardless of what happens to them here. This is very important for us as Christians to remember when we encounter government oppression in any form. The king and his officers are God's ministers, accountable to Him.

:10-15 The closing passage of this section of Ecclesiastes focuses on the guarantee that God will bring justice in the next life even if injustice prevails under the sun. This section of the Preacher's argument supports his overall theme by explaining why life under the sun does not appear to be under God's control. If God made us and gave us this life for our good, why are so many wicked, miserable, or oppressed by others? The answer is twofold: first, man sins and corrupts the good things God gives; second, God is in control anyway and will deliver justice in the next life.

Evil people do not last long, because no people last long. The vapor of life is an assurance that the wicked will not get away with anything they do. To die is to go before God. Verses 12 and 13 could be no more explicit in declaring that this life is not the end. A long-lived sinner has accomplished nothing. His years have merely served to heap up eternal punishments. Those who fear God will be well, even if they die earlier than the wicked.

On earth, everything is vapor, whether it is right or wrong. Only under the sun do men treat a righteous man like a wicked man and vice-versa. Beyond the sun, God will treat all of us as we are in His sight—whether we feared Him or not. Remember that fear manifests faith, faith in God that results in salvation.

Therefore, do not think it unusual or shocking when the righteous suffer and human beings are evil. The proper response for anyone, much more the child of God, is to eat and drink and be merry because pleasure is the gift of God. This expresses an attitude of trust. A Christian who enjoys life as God's gift in spite of hardship expresses trust in God. Sinners worry and fret. Worry is a sin because God is in sovereign control. Enjoy your life and labor in the face of the world's endless anxieties. No sooner has one problem disappeared than another takes its place. The fallen world will always worry about pollution, or crime, or energy reserves, or the economy, or social programs, or whatever. These things matter to a Christian to the extent they matter to God. But to unregenerate minds these and other problems are all that matters. Life under the sun is horrible without God.

Review and Discussion

1. Why is a good reputation important? Who is affected by your reputation besides you?

2. List some reasons why it is better to think about the day of your death than it is to think about the party you have planned for next Saturday.

3. Explain how the "long view" of life changes a person's attitude toward each of the following:

   Money

   A new job

   College

   Death

4. When I was in high school, a very popular girl a couple of years older than I was died suddenly in the middle of the year, and the yearbook gave a dedication to her on its last page. Let's suppose that a friend of yours was killed in a car accident this year. The editor of your school yearbook wants to make the last page a memorial to her, and asks you to write a short dedication for it on the text, "the house of feasting and the house of mourning" from Ecclesiastes. Write a rough draft of what you might say below.

5. How could you be "excessively wicked" in regards to your daily clothing?

6. Why does the Preacher use a woman as the embodiment of human failure?

7. What should be your response to a man who, believing passionately that your local mayor is corrupt and needs to be ejected from office, tries to enlist your aid in inciting civil disobedience against the mayor's order that no church can set up a booth at the town fall festival?

8. What is a simple response to someone who wonders, angrily, why some good Christian leader dies of cancer in the prime of his life when other public leaders, known to be ungodly, live on, healthy and actively promoting evil?

Overview

Wisdom is paramount but human failure persists. 7:1-29

Wisdom Poem—The long-range view of life 7:1-14

Wisdom demands moderation and fairness. 7:15-25

Wisdom does not prevent human failure. 7:26-29

Wisdom is paramount but life is transient. 8:1-15

Wisdom demands respect for God-ordained authority. 8:1-9

Justice and injustice are both transient. 8:10-14

Conclusion: Enjoy good things to sustain you, but don't consider them the absolute solution to life. 8:15 (Epicurean
Refrain)

CHAPTER SIX

This Slippery, Tricky Life We Live

6

Memory Verses: Ecclesiastes 9:9, 10:1

8:16 Verse 16 of Chapter 8 begins what we will consider the fifth division of Ecclesiastes. An "Epicurean refrain" in 8:15 closed the previous section. Now the Preacher repeats what he found on his quest—no one can explore all the work of God, however much time, energy, and money he expends.

Remember the original audience of this book and put yourself in their place. It will not be difficult, because you probably have much in common with them—young, educated, able, and at the point of departure into your own life. The Preacher becomes very pointed here about the nature of life: regardless of how good and industrious you think you are, you will die just like every other man.

Realize that your relationship to God makes a dramatic difference in how you will respond to these straightforward declarations. If you don't know God, you resent it. If you fear God, you glorify and thank Him both for making this life worthwhile and for giving you another life that is far, far better. He will not leave you in a world of bitter hardship and frequent injustice. Look beyond the sun.

One Fate

9:1-6 The first six verses of Chapter 9 are another difficult section. If you dropped into the middle of Ecclesiastes and read these without knowing the context of the book, what would you think? In isolation, these verses could sound like a denial of eternal life. By now, you realize that it is a confession of God's sovereign control and an admonition to avoid resting your hopes in this life. He does not mean that God looks on all people the same; instead, he means that they all look the same to us. Sacrifices and oaths were external signs of religion.

Destiny of the Dead

Think About It!

Ecclesiastes 9:4-6 certainly seems to be a problem for Christians. Since so much of our emphasis is upon the joys of heaven, these verses are disconcerting. We believe the Bible says that when any person dies, his soul goes to either heaven or hell and is there fully conscious and aware (Luke 16). Verse 5 could be taken to mean that the dead are oblivious.

But notice that verse 6 says in plain language that this is an observation "under the sun." Much of Ecclesiastes looks at the world under the sun. It does not mean that Solomon was denying an afterlife; rather, he just isn't referring to the afterlife. It is as if a Christian preacher were to say, "When you die, it's all over." Taken out of context, such a statement sounds like death results in oblivion. But you know that most preachers would mean that death ends a person's chances to trust Christ as Savior. Hence, "it's all over" at death for Christians and non-Christians alike.

You can draw parallels to people in your own church. Some people work hard for the church, giving their time, money, and energy to serving others. Some people are very careful to keep high standards and avoid worldliness, while others are less concerned about appearances and associations. I hope no one in your church is outright wicked, but some churches have such people—some churches are full of them, in fact. All of them die. Death is therefore the most significant event in life because it is the one unavoidable equivocator of all human beings. Death results from sin. No one is good enough to avoid death. Do you see why Ecclesiastes has the force of a tract? It speaks to everyone in the world, everyone in any age in history. Every human life is a vapor.

:7 The correct response to the state of life is to enjoy the good in it. If life under the sun were all there is, there would be no reason to enjoy it. But God's presence makes life worth enjoying. God has already approved the works of man because God created man and gave man his works.

Notice how this points the reader to God. Imagine someone reading this book who knew nothing of the true God. He is devoted to worldliness, caught up unknowingly in the pursuit of vain things, and doomed to eternal death. The Preacher has proclaimed the futility of finding satisfaction in life but now declares that God can make it possible to enjoy life! The imperative is to choose joy, but the reason is that God has made life for His own purposes. You must set your heart on Him to live like a human is supposed to.

While it may appear that the gospel is absent from Ecclesiastes, the fact is that it meets unsaved people where they are and turns their minds away from the world and onto God. The genius of the book, as with all biblical wisdom literature, is that it speaks effectively to both the godly and ungodly. It speaks to the individual about matters relevant to all of us, whatever our spiritual state.

:8 White clothes are the sign of festivity, in contrast to mourning clothes. Recall the Preacher's emphasis on the importance of funerals (7:2-4). Do these verses contradict? Only if we make the assumption that death invariably causes grief. To the Preacher, death is a grief only to those who do not know God. Sobriety about death does not have to lead to depression; on the contrary, death is no terror to one who fears God and looks to Him for life.

:9 Wisdom literature teaches young people how to live a whole life that pleases God. One key to a godly life is the right marriage. Solomon knew about profligacy; he is notorious for having a thousand wives and concubines over his lifetime. But his counsel to the young man is to enjoy life with *the* woman he loves throughout his entire life. Joy in marriage is a deliberate, continual choice, but it is God's great gift. One man and one woman for one lifetime is God's will and God's best. Moral purity leads to joy above any worldly indulgence. Life wears out the sinner until he cannot even take natural pleasure in the flesh, but God gives lifetime joy to those who fear and obey him.

:10 Sheol, the grave, is a proper name in the Old Testament for the abode of the dead. It is used for the grave, literally and figura-

tively, and occasionally for the place of departed spirits. All people who die go to Sheol as surely as all Christians who die go to the cemetery. The souls of people in Sheol have gone to the spirit world, either heaven or hell (Luke 16:19-31).

However, the opportunities afforded by this life do not extend to Sheol. Heaven is far better than earth, but heaven is not in question in verse 10. It is another reminder that death overtakes us all. God's gift of life must not be taken for granted. He is pleased when we do all we can to the best of our abilities, for that is the reason He gave us life.

Furthermore, give your all to life without expecting perfect justice and equity. Conventional wisdom would dictate that, if life is unfair, why should I love life? The Preacher wants me to be swift, strong, wise, and capable if I can be, but tells me that I may not be successful anyway! This would be ridiculous if life under the sun were all there is. But with God to be the ultimate arbiter and rewarder, I can undertake all my labor with full zeal even without earthly reward because I know that He will reward me in the next life. As for these human beings who deny me fairness and equity, they will all go down to Sheol in due time and eventually go before God.

:11-12 Live with this fact in mind: life will eventually do you in. God would not be doing you a favor by keeping that fact secret if it is true. Accept your mortality and act accordingly. Live life joyfully but aware of God and what He demands.

When you read of some scientist trying to find the key to eternal life, you can be sure it is a vain hope. God has set few limits on what mankind may accomplish through science. He made only death inevitable. Scientists do not understand even the "reasons" for aging. Perhaps science will advance various explanations over time, but we can be sure they will never find the way to prevent death. All human beings long for eternal life, but only God can give it.

:13-18 We don't know if this incident is from somewhere else in Scripture, but most likely it is not. Solomon probably had a real historical event in mind, but part of his point is its obscurity—it is an incredible story, but hardly anyone has heard it.

The incident Solomon relates presents wisdom at its very best from an earthly point of view. One would think that even ungodly people would be so overwhelmed with awe and gratitude toward the wise man that saved their city that they would exalt him, honor him, make a statue of him, write ballads about him, make a biographical movie, and in all other ways immortalize his name.

But that did not happen. Not only have you and I never heard of this old wise man, but even three thousand years ago they had forgotten him. The point, made often before in Ecclesiastes (1:17-18; 2:15, 21), is this: wisdom is vastly superior to folly in getting things done, but the damage done by sin both ruins what wisdom gains and erases its memory. Even wisdom is vapor.

10:1 One of life's tough ironies is that a man who is otherwise noble and good can look bad because of a single flaw. Remember that "foolishness" is not mere ignorance or clumsiness, but what we call a character flaw. Imagine a pastor who is a good preacher, a wise counselor, and a brave leader, but short-tempered. Are you not likely to think more often of one negative trait than three positive ones? A quick temper is not wise, and it can make a very good man lose credibility.

:3 How much more glaring is it when a man is altogether foolish! Even simple activities reveal foolishness. It should be obvious that wisdom and folly characterize a man's whole life. One's actions, choices, speech, and company fall in line according to one's wisdom.

:4 Verse 4 gives an excellent illustration of the difference wisdom makes. This is something you need to remember: when an important person—say an employer, a school administrator, or a judge—becomes angry at you over a position you have taken, show wisdom. A fool's response is either to backpedal and deny his position or to lose his own temper in turn. Neither will be helpful. Remember that this is a king writing. He was used to challenging people about things they had said or done. His counsel is to stay composed and hold your ground. When people see calm certainty, they respect you. This assumes you are sure of yourself; of course, if you find yourself to be truly in the wrong, humbly acknowledge your mistake and ask forgiveness. But if you are sure you are right, do not get combative, do not lie, and do not change your stance just to please men. Most authority figures can see through a façade, anyway. Wisdom shows that you have maturity, self-restraint, and character.

Your Turn

:5-7 You are probably able to describe the purpose of verses 5-7. What theme do they continue? Write your answer in the blank provided at the end of this lesson (question #4).

:8-11 The next verses should also sound familiar. The Preacher nears the close of his discourse and puts the final tiles in place in his mosaic of interlocking themes. For this section, I will give you some notes to make it clear what the Preacher is talking about. You write what the proverbs mean and relate "wisdom" to their overall meaning.

If you had lived back then, you might dig a pit to be a cistern or well. Leviticus provides penalties for leaving a pit uncovered if an animal or person fell into it.

The wall breaker was not being destructive. The wall is of piled stones, probably mortared with mud. These walls acted as boundaries for vineyards or fields. Knocking one down meant you were enlarging the field to grow larger crops, so it was a constructive thing to do.

Likewise, quarrying stones and splitting wood are industrious activities. Verse 10 states, oh so profoundly, that a sharp ax ("iron") makes it easier to chop wood. Verse 11 is not talking about a magician, but a practitioner of the familiar (if uninviting) Near Eastern practice of snake charming, apparently a legitimate pursuit in Solomon's Israel.

:12-15 You should be able to handle these verses just as well. Without being too personal, write a description of someone you know (without using the name) who exemplifies verses 13-14. Now consider, do you also exemplify that description? Are you endlessly talking about things of no substance? Remember, this is a mark of a fool, not a wise person.

Verse 15 is difficult. It seems to say that a fool so destroys himself that he cannot even walk to a city. It is hard to catch the image, but you get the point.

:16-18 The discussion of folly turns to the dangers of laziness. The word "princes" does not designate only the king's sons, but all of the chief rulers in a country. They could well be older than the king, just as in verse 16. When a child becomes king, he lacks the skill and experience to maintain control. Even if he is a good boy, he will not be a good king until he matures. The image of princes eating, or feasting, in the morning conveys an atmosphere full of irresponsibility. These rulers abuse their position to indulge their appetites. Wise rulers do not misuse their power or their God-given desire for pleasure. Remember that Ecclesiastes was originally a book for young people preparing for positions of responsibility, usually in the government. Whether or not you work in government, the fact that you are receiving a formal education means that you have the capacity to be a ruler in some area, such as your business, church, or community. Be a wise ruler. Be diligent to control yourself and do not indulge in self-gratification.

:20 We'll note this verse out of order because it echoes earlier verses, such as because somehow, sooner or later, they will get back to the ears of the person you are criticizing. If the Preacher seems disjointed here, don't blame it on senility. He is drawing to the close of his book, and the cyclical style leads him to switch rapidly from topic to topic in order to reinforce them one last time before he reaches his conclusion. It has been a challenge to say everything he wanted to in balanced form. Verse 19 attaches to Chapter 11, so we will look at it in the next chapter.

Review and Discussion

1. Is the gospel in Ecclesiastes? Explain your answer.

2. If I am guaranteed to die, and if I am not guaranteed to succeed in things I attempt on this life, on what basis do I put any sincere effort into my work and ministry?

3. What is the point of accumulating wisdom, as Ecclesiastes defines wisdom?

4. Summarize the meaning of Ecclesiastes 10:5-7.

*O*verview

Life is transient. 8:16–9:10

> God has made man unable to find satisfaction in earthly life.
> 8:16–9:1

> Life is transient for all men, good and bad. 9:2-6

> Conclusion: Be joyful in this life. 9:7-10

Wisdom is paramount but inadequate due to sin. 9:11–11:6

> Wisdom is paramount but often unappreciated and consumed
> by injustice. 9:11-18

> Wisdom is paramount but cannot reverse human failures.
> 10:1-20

CHAPTER SEVEN

Rejoice and Remember

7

Memory Verses: Ecclesiastes 11:9-10 and 12:1

The Preacher approaches the conclusion to his book with a final flurry of wisdom proverbs teaching young people how to map out a successfully God-honoring life. Some of these closing admonitions sound more spiritual than the rest. Some sound almost worldly. But all of them are "spiritual" in the sense that they are God's will for our lives. We must take them in balance, not seeing more than is there and not acting as if Ecclesiastes exists in isolation from the rest of Scripture.

Money Matters

10:19 We will pick up verse 19 and bring it together with 11:1-4. These verses transmit basic principles of finance. Life under the sun necessarily involves money. Beyond the sun, money is irrelevant, just as it would have been on earth had man never sinned. But while we fear and follow God through mortal life, finance is one of the vapors we must understand and use.

Verse 19 contributes by putting money in perspective among life's pleasures: food and drink offer some physical satisfaction, but money meets every need. Please do not think he implies money can buy love or salvation or peace of mind. The realm in view is physical need. Money is the means to provide for physical needs during life. This is not to say one never lives a life of faith. It does not say to live life for money. Solomon merely makes the undeniable observation that money is the means for earthly provision. Sin is actually responsible for making money necessary, because sin caused the curse on the earth and its resulting scarcity, which requires men to work for their food. But sin is the problem, not money.

Chapter 11 starts with some applications in view of the importance of money. The Lord does not make many Christians wealthy (by worldly standards) because few of us could handle it humbly.

We tend to rely on wealth instead of God, but that is not because wealth is evil. God is absolutely wealthy (Psalm 24:1). He intends for us to use money for certain things. So how do I get money God's way?

11:1-2 Verse 1 often appears in exhortations to spread the gospel around. It is good to spread the gospel, but do not stop with eight people. In context with verse 2, this is clearly a principle for investments. As any sensible secular investment counselor will tell you, *diversify*. When you are young, start setting money aside for a small portfolio of investments for the purpose of financial security. No matter your income, you can carve out a small percentage for savings. Do not bury it all in the ground, but spread it around in wise investments so that it will multiply itself. Avoid excessive risk as well as insufficient risk. Consider a variety of recipients, including banks, bonds, businesses, stocks, and funds. Look toward long-term, not short-term, goals. Solomon is not suggesting a get-rich-quick scheme, but a wise way of providing for yourself and your family in days to come.

:3-6 Investment diversity guards against unforeseeable disaster. The smartest broker on earth does not know what the future holds. Weather, economics, wars, and social change will all continue under the sun. Do not be afraid to act; remember that all is

in God's hands. Take life's financial ups and downs in stride, staying diligent and faithful. Do you see that this attitude is the opposite of the "love of money"? On the contrary, this is the life of faith. Labor is a gift, but a gift that brings rewards. Being lazy shows that I do not appreciate God's gifts and that I presume upon His blessings. Faithfully laboring through times of plenty and times of want shows that I trust him to care for me and that I believe obedience to His will eventually pays off. I acknowledge my dependence on Him and increase my appreciation for the time when I can rest from the toil of life.

Closing In

:7-9 From 11:7 to the end, the Preacher draws his final applications. This is what he wants you, the reader, to do. He has written many things for you to know, but now he writes the part about what to do in light of what you know. He has hinted earlier at these applications, and now they come to fruition. Are you prepared to grasp all of Ecclesiastes as a whole and obey its directions for your life?

Based on the opening theme of Ecclesiastes, "All is vapor," what would you expect the Preacher's closing application to young men to be? If this were a depressing, pessimistic book, I would expect him to be fatalistic. Perhaps he would tell me to do what I want when I want how I want because life is short (echoing certain modern advertising slogans).

On the other hand, if this were a book of rigorous duty to a fearsome, judgmental God, I would expect the last application to urge diligent obedience to God's commands. I would expect an exaltation of duty, discipline, and self-denial.

This entire book has been about life under the sun, where labor is long, justice is short, and nothing is permanent. But what says the first verse in the Preacher's closing? That it is good and *pleasant* to see the sun! From the proper, godly perspective, life is enjoyable. He does not mean that this life is all there is, but that this life is still good despite all the damage caused by sin.

Verse 8 begins a string of critically important verses. Two key words in this section are *rejoice* and *remember*. Both are imperatives; we choose to obey them or not. To rejoice is to choose joy, to decide to be happy. To remember is to call to mind or contemplate something, not just memorize. Keep these definitions in mind as you read the rest of Ecclesiastes.

The first line of verse 8 speaks for itself. Think through everything that the Preacher has said about life and try to balance it all in your mind at once. Life under the sun is full of apparently ceaseless repetition that never results in any permanent accomplishment. We humans have an innate desire for something permanently satisfying, but no earthly endeavor is enough. However,

God put that desire in us for the ultimate purpose of directing us to Him because only He can fill it. In the meantime, God shows His goodness by giving us regular portions of temporarily satisfying things, like food and drink. God wants us to enjoy life. With wisdom, the skill of doing His will in daily life, we will be joyful even during our pilgrimage under the sun. The blessings of the eternal life are not in view, but are assumed by the Preacher as the basis for obedience and happiness in this life.

Consequently, the exhortation in 11:8 makes good sense. But what are "the days of darkness"? They are not death. It makes no sense to "remember" all the days that you will be dead or to point out that they will be numerous. The Preacher has already declared that, from our human perspective, the grave is the end. Moreover, Chapter 12 will use the imagery of darkness to picture old age. It is most likely that old age is the "days of darkness," the wane of earthly life that forces us to reflect on the life we have led and face the fact of our own mortality and the fast-approaching end of life. Hence the last phrase of verse 8, a poignant reminder that everything in your life is vapor.

Remember

Verse 9 gives one of two commands that, combined, encapsulate the message from God to us in Ecclesiastes. Young men are to rejoice, to choose joy, while they are still young. It seems so simplistic, and not overly spiritual. Yet it is both highly spiritual and deeply profound when you realize how much it takes to obey this command. No lost people and few Christians know true joy. Those that do tend to be advanced in years before they become genuinely joyful. But God's will, God's command, is to be joyful in youth.

Godly joy does not preclude sorrow for sin, grief at loss, a serious mindset, or occasional regret. It does preclude depression, worry, bitterness, and that deep-seated anger some people hold against God, their families, the whole world, or whatever. All these are sins. They reveal a failure to know God that causes rebellion against Him.

Unsaved people can seem happy. Indeed, they are happy at times thanks to God's abundant generosity even to those who do not know Him or thank Him. But no one without God possesses the joy He commands. People have to live in a state of denial or self-deception to be happy without God. But God's will for us is not toil or drudgery. It is not asceticism. It is not a life of bravely suffering for God when you would have preferred not to.

No, God's will is joy. But godly joy makes its Author its object of highest affection and sole source of satisfaction. Whether you live with little or much, you will be joyful. If you live long or short, you will be joyful. Giving things up for God is not a sacrifice because you already have the greatest, most fulfilling treasure a human being ever possesses. You have God.

The Preacher's admonition to follow your heart and the desires of the eyes may sound like dangerous advice. After all, are not Christians supposed to avoid lust and covetousness? Of course they are, but by now you know to think hard about what the Preacher means in context of his whole book. You know that fulfilling your natural human desires is not wrong when it is done as God intended. This is precisely the reason for the final sentence of 11:9.

Judgment here is not in the sense of condemnation, but of evaluation. Remember God while you enjoy life. Consider His Word: does this choice or that one please Him? Will you glorify Him by this course of action? It is necessary to think of God's eventual judgment if you are to make right decisions that lead to a joyful life. You must live aware of God in order to be joyful, and the result of living aware of God is a life of joy.

On the daily level, verse 9 shows that your innate desires may very well lead you in God's will for your future. Young people normally wonder what to do with their lives. Along with the choice of your marriage partner, choosing your life calling is the most important decision you ever make. Be comforted that you may not be called on to make this decision until you are much older. Few people know in their teen years what to give their lives to. Most college graduates eventually do something other than what they majored in. It may take delving into two or three alternatives before God reveals your life's work. One place to look for guidance is, very simply, at what you want to do. Natural aptitude and inclination are excellent guides; after all, God made no mistake when He assembled you and orchestrated your childhood experiences. Do not be afraid to pursue your heart's desires, but do so constantly aware of God and His Word. Whatever He calls you to, be it homemaker or missionary or engineer, it will be the most joyful occupation possible.

:10 You might think that God's coming judgment would be a reason to fear and tremble, but the Preacher makes it a reason for young people to rid themselves of all sorrow and pain. Many young people are inwardly miserable. This is sin. It is against God's will, and leads to disaster. Certainly many young people have good reason to be miserable because they have been badly injured by sin, theirs and others'. But no wound is too great for the power of God to heal. Joy is choosing to be happy through the power of God on the basis of what God has done in Jesus Christ. Your youth is the time in which you set the tone and course of your entire life. Get that fact and remember it. Youth is vapor; it is a brief and limited time. Once gone it is gone for eternity, for you are an immortal being. Reincarnation is not possible. You get only one youth to live God's way.

12:1 Along with "Rejoice in your youth," the first line of Chapter 12 summarizes the Preacher's message to every young person. *Remember* means "to think on." Consider that for a moment. It takes a conscious effort to stay aware of God. Spend the effort to think about God all the time of your youth and it will guide you in your choices. Your whole life will take shape according to the foundation you lay in early years—your values, your life's goals, and your basic abilities.

Though we often think of God as our Creator, verse 1 is one of only three places in the Old Testament where that title occurs for God. There is a reason Solomon used it there. Throughout Ecclesiastes there has been a close connection to the creation account in Genesis. The endless cycle of natural activity, life "under the sun," and the results of the fall of man all echo the earliest events in Genesis. The fact that God created you and the world in which you live implies several things. For one, He has the right to tell you what to do. For another, He knows far better than anyone else how His creation functions, whether winds, animals, or human souls. And one more blessed fact: He who created all things has the power to create them all again. Your soul is corrupted by sin, but the Creator can regenerate it. You are bound for eternal death, but the Creator can give new life. Your body will decay and die, but the Creator can make for you a new body free from the transitory nature of this world.

The time in view in Ecclesiastes 12 is old age. As always, we have to understand the Preacher's words in context with the rest of his book and the rest of Scripture. Elsewhere Solomon praises the wisdom of the elderly (as in Prov. 16:31). But here his focus is on the end of earthly life. You and I are vapor while we live under the sun. Our ability to enjoy life and serve God is limited by our mortality. Remember God while you are still young so that your whole life will go God's way.

Some young people have the temptation to think they will get serious about religion when they are older, usually so that they can "have fun" now. This is foolish for at least three reasons. First, life at any age is more "fun" with God than apart from Him. Second, wasting youth steals the most productive and appropriate time to learn about and serve God. Even if a person turns to God late in life, he has given away what cannot be regained. Third, putting fleshly desires before the Lord normally reveals an unregenerate heart. An unsaved young person will not become a godly old person. Such a one has no fear of the Lord.

Effects of Old Age

:2 Verses 2-7 are a poem describing the effects of decay in old age. Our ability to enjoy the life God gives fades as we age. We cannot say for sure what all of these images represent, but the overall picture is clear enough. These are poetic images of reality. Imagine the sounds and sights described and think about what points of similarity to aging the Preacher has in mind.

Darkness is a general symbol of fading life and energy. Clouds are fluffy white, like the whitened hair of the elderly.

:3 The "watchmen" are probably the legs and back, which lose strength and become tremulous. The "house" image for the human body appears several times in this poem.

Grinders were people who milled grain into bread. Most likely they stand for our teeth, which fall out and wear down as we age. "Those that look out of the windows" probably refers to the eyes. Notice the connection to the theme of eating earlier in the book. Old age, "the dark days," removes our ability to enjoy earthly life.

:4 This verse appears to relate to loss of hearing. Many of life's joys consist partly of sound, but the world falls increasingly silent as one ages. "He shall rise up at the voice of the bird" shows that older people are easily startled.

:5 Older people tend to fear falling because their bones are brittle and heal slowly. This sort of infirmity reduces a man's capacity for new experiences and adventures that once fulfilled him. Almond trees bloom white all over, like

a head of white hair. The last two sentences refer to the reduction of sexual desire.

Man's real home is beyond the sun. King Solomon wants to get the attention of all young people, godly and ungodly. All must face death.

:6 I do not know what specific things the images in verse 6 represent. Scholars have given various suggestions, but all of them express the failure of various mechanisms to function properly.

All of the body's systems weaken and fail as the years pile up. No one has ever explained why we age. Medical science may propose different explanations, but the fact is that no one can really explain why human beings—or any other organism for that matter—weaken and die when they have plenty of air, food, and water. Why are we born growing, but even as we grow begin to show signs of age? The true cause, whatever intermediary factors we may identify, is sin. Sin brings death (Rom. 6:23). God did not wish death on us; we sin and bring death on ourselves.

:7 Our bodies are nothing but animated mud. I may be buried in a fancy coffin, but my body will rot just the same. In the meantime, my spirit will go beyond the sun to its Creator.

:8 The Preacher summarizes his theme just as he began (1:2). This is a very emphatic statement: all is vapor. This life under the sun, this very world in which we live, is a mere breath.

Epilogue

:9 Verses 9-14 are the epilogue or conclusion to Ecclesiastes. His main arguments complete, Solomon looks upon the whole work to offer closing advice to his readers. He will make bold claims in this conclusion, claims that set his book above other wisdom writings in the ancient Near East. Finally, he will summarize the Lord's message to all of us one last time.

:10 While the Preacher gives us a good example to follow by sharing his wisdom with others, his main point is that what we have just read is a product of his wisdom. We have here great testimony to the miracle of inspiration. Solomon did not merely sit and spill out all these words as if he were taking dictation. He labored in his mind to understand the way of life and to write in such a way that young readers could learn wisdom.

:11 The dual image in verse 11 of goads and nails gives the impression that wise words force us in certain directions. Goads are pointed wooden sticks used to drive cattle. The nails could refer to metal nails that hold a structure together or to the nail at the tip of a goad that made it even sharper (and more painful to the cattle). As you remember from the introduction, the one Shepherd who gives the words of the wise is certainly God. Solomon has no reason to refer to himself as the one shepherd who gives all the words of the wise. He was the wisest man, but not the only wise man.

:12 Verse 12 is yet another verse anyone in school should treasure. But we have to keep in mind what it means in context. The Preacher's warning is about trying to find the same answers to ultimate questions or give meaning and happiness to life. God has revealed Himself as the ultimate answer in such a way that anyone can get it. Mankind acts as if he could figure out the answers, given enough time and energy. But God already gave the answers to us freely, a long time ago.

:13-14 The final poem of Ecclesiastes summarizes what we have to do. Remember everything included in the fear of God—it is the same as saying, "Remember God." This is the whole of man, everything there is to human existence. More than just duty, it is our purpose and our ultimate joy. God's coming judgment is a terror only to those who oppose Him. To those who fear, love, obey, and enjoy Him, it is the guarantee of eternal life and fulfillment—beyond the sun.

Review and Discussion

1. Compare what the Preacher advises about money in Ecclesiastes 11:1-6 with what the Apostle Paul wrote in I Timothy 6:6-10. Why do these passages not contradict?

2. Write the two key words in the application section of Ecclesiastes and briefly define what they mean.

3. Why should a young man "remember the days of darkness"? Explain what that phrase means and how it applies to young people.

4. Explain why doing what you want to do is a potentially legitimate way of discerning God's leading for your life.

5. Suppose you have two young nephews. One of them thinks God wants him to be a missionary in the darkest, deepest African jungle he can find. He is thrilled about it, being an outdoors sort of kid who loves weird bugs. Your other nephew says that God wants him to be a missionary to African jungles, too, but he seems really worried about it. He doesn't really like the woods, and he positively despises bugs. What can you tell your second nephew about the will of God?

6. Why do our bodies wear out as we age and finally die?

Overview

Wisdom with wealth makes life enjoyable. 11:1-6

Climax—Because earthly life is inadequate to satisfy, even with wisdom, but is still God's gift to draw us closer to Himself, choose joy while you are still young and live aware of God from your youth onward. 11:7–12:1

Old age removes the ability to enjoy earthly life and serve God with your body. 12:2-8

Conclusion—Because God is in absolute control and will judge everyone, fear God! This is the *whole* of man. 12:9-14

Notes

Notes

Notes

Notes

Notes

Photograph Credits

The following agencies and individuals have furnished materials to meet the photographic needs of this textbook. We wish to express our gratitude to them for their important contribution.

British Official Photography
Doug Garland
Dr. Stewart Custer
Photodisc
Tara Swaney
www.arttoday.com

Introduction Page
Illustration by Gustave Dore iv

Chapter 1
Photodisc 1

Chapter 2
Dr. Stewart Custer 26; Photodisc 30, 31 (surrounding ovals); Tara Swaney 31 (center inset)

Chapter 4
British Official Photography 54; Tara Swaney 57 (top left); www.arttoday.com 57 (middle and bottom)

Chapter 6
Doug Garland 83